William Bradner Slaughter

The modern Genesis

Being an Inquiry into the Credibility of the Nebular Theory, of the Origin of

planetary Bodies, etc.

William Bradner Slaughter

The modern Genesis
Being an Inquiry into the Credibility of the Nebular Theory, of the Origin of planetary Bodies, etc.

ISBN/EAN: 9783337138967

Printed in Europe, USA, Canada, Australia, Japan

Cover: Foto ©ninafisch / pixelio.de

More available books at **www.hansebooks.com**

THE MODERN GENESIS.

BEING

AN INQUIRY INTO THE CREDIBILITY OF THE NEBULAR THEORY, OF THE ORIGIN OF PLANETARY BODIES, THE STRUCTURE OF THE SOLAR SYSTEM, AND OF GENERAL COSMICAL HISTORY.

BY REV. W. B. SLAUGHTER.

Progress consists in this, that with the increase of knowledge, the conceptions which have sprung from the imagination vanish; and while, in the first periods of science, this faculty has undisputed ascendency, at a later stage it subordinates itself to the understanding, and becomes, to the latter, a helpful and willing servant.—*Baron Von Liebig.*

NEW YORK:
NELSON & PHILLIPS.
CINCINNATI:
HITCHCOCK & WALDEN.
1876.

Entered according to Act of Congress, in the year 1876, by

NELSON & PHILLIPS,

in the Office of the Librarian of Congress at Washington.

PREFACE.

IN the following pages the nebular theory is discussed simply as a theory of modern science. Whatever relation it may bear to the account of the creation given by Moses, and referred to by other sacred writers, the author has chosen to ignore it altogether in his treatment of the subject. A scientific question must be settled on scientific grounds only. No other treatment can be satisfactory to thinking men.

The title, THE MODERN GENESIS, is thought to be appropriate, as the nebular theory is a modern theory of the origin or worlds.

That the advocates of this theory will spare the arguments herein presented is not to be expected, nor, indeed, desired. Truth being the object of our search, we shall welcome it though it come through the ruins of our own fabric. It may be objected by some that we seek to overthrow a theory, yet do not advance a better one to take its place. It will be a sufficient answer to say that the sublime statements, "In the beginning God created the heaven and the earth;" that "he spake, and it was done; he commanded, and it stood fast," embody about all the theory that to us appears to possess any certainty, and we give to this our reverent assent. Beyond this statement there is little but very uncertain speculation. Geological data may suffice for a limited terrestrial history, but, we think, fall infinitely short of the necessities of a cosmical history. Nor do the cognate sciences furnish data sufficient for such a history.

That the whole field may be re-examined, and definite truth be reached as the result of the publication of this unpretending volume, is the sincere wish of THE AUTHOR.

LINCOLN, NEBRASKA, *October* 25, 1875.

CONTENTS.

Chapter	Page
I. Introduction	7
II. The Nebular Hypothesis	17
III. Cause of Rotary Motion	34
IV. Ring Formations	55
V. Actual Velocities	75
VI. Direction of Planetary Motions	88
VII. Densities	117
VIII. Densities—Continued	132
IX. Planetary History	143
X. Terrestrial Changes	163
XI. The Moon	191
XII. The Sun	210
XIII. Temperature of the Planets	235
XIV. Physical Condition of Mars	264
XV. Planetary Masses	276

THE MODERN GENESIS.

CHAPTER I.

INTRODUCTION.

So long as the phenomena of nature continue to be the subject of human observation, so long will the human mind busy itself with questions of cause.

But the question of cause once raised, there is no end to the inquiry; for, back of the immediate cause of any phenomenon a remoter cause will be sought; and, if that be found, another still beyond will be sought; until a final cause of all will be demanded. Thus, ever searching; ever gratified with new discoveries, yet never fully satisfied; the instinct of curiosity and the nobler love of truth unite to make man the unwearied explorer of all the realms of nature.

The results are, first, the accumulation of a

vast mass of independent facts; and, afterward, the grouping of these facts into departments of correlated data, out of which are constructed systems of science.

A sublime pleasure rewards the discoverer. The discovery of a law of nature must be attended with emotions not less exquisite than those which thrill the heart of him who discovers a world.

In either case the joy will be the greater because the law and the world are old; for he who alone, of all the millions of his own age and the millions of past ages, perceives a truth which was equally a truth before, and was equally open to them all, is worthy of higher distinction than he who is the first to perceive, because he is favored with the first opportunity.

Perhaps a higher talent is requisite to arrange discovered facts into systems of science, than to make the discoveries; yet the number of those who have theorized abundantly is far greater than the number of those who have made important discoveries.

It has been the misfortune of science that the genius of generalization has often outrun the patient gatherer of well-authenticated *data;* and thus theories have gained general acceptance as scientific truth for a season, only to be disavowed in subsequent times and replaced by other theories.

In nothing, perhaps, does modern science differ more from ancient science, than in its habit of testing theories by a rigid comparison with known facts.

An original thinker may be in danger of becoming an erratic thinker; and, indeed, he is, if he do not constantly bind and limit himself by established truths.

Because fancies are often mistaken for facts he who theorizes ought to be not only assured of his facts, but able also to appeal to them as facts known and acknowledged by scientific men. Moreover, it is needful that all the known facts that bear on the subject of his theory shall be consulted, and their testimony taken.

In no scientific inquiry should the scientist play the partisan. He who argues in support of a theory because the theory, if sustained, will support a theology, is incapacitated by his bias for equitably weighing facts.

He who advocates a theory because it is

hostile to a theology is equally unfitted for impartial investigation, and is quite as likely to embrace an error as to find a truth.

Science is knowledge; not fancy; not hypothesis. And yet fancy may precede hypothesis, and hypothesis may become the formula of confirmed scientific truth. As a hypothesis, it must be subject to the ordeal of comparison with known facts, and if it abide this ordeal, then it may be installed as a doctrine of science.

The old theory, that "The earth is the center of the universe, and all the heavenly bodies revolve around it," was a hypothesis which could not abide the test of observed facts, and it passed away.

That the sun is the center of our planetary system was at first deemed but a wild fancy. Reflection clothed it with the details of a highly probable hypothesis; and the careful observation of the heavenly bodies, aided by instruments of great delicacy and power, at length gave to the hypothesis the authority of established truth.

The general structure of the solar system is no longer the subject of debate.

Such, in brief, as the following, are now universally admitted astronomical facts.

The sun is the center of the system. The planets revolve around the sun in elliptical orbits. Around some of the primary planets, secondary planets or moons also revolve in elliptical orbits, and accompany the primary around the sun. The sun revolves on its axis. Each of the planets (except two, which are *supposed* to have a similar motion) revolves on its axis. The general direction of planetary motion is from west to east.

The periods of planetary revolution are mathematically related to their respective distances from the sun. The sun is the source of light and heat to the planets, each of which shines with reflected light. Even to the naked eye some of these grand movements of the heavenly bodies are perceptible. The planet Venus vibrates in the heavens, alternately the evening and the morning star.

The moon from evening to evening advances to new positions among the stars, and Mars, Jupiter, and Saturn move slowly forward among the constellations. And thus it has been from age to age.

Gazing with admiring wonder on these glorious objects, how many have asked, "What are they? What is that sun? What are those moving lights? What are those fixed stars? What power upholds them? What guides have those wanderers amid those distant wastes? And whence are they? How did they come into being? Has each a history? What is that history?"

And how *few* of the generations that have passed away were able to answer even the simplest of these questions with satisfaction to themselves.

Of cosmical theories there have been many, and yet there is no discouragement of that curious intelligence which devotes itself to cosmical study. Indeed, never before did the human mind explore the universe with so much eagerness in search of facts, out of which to construct a cosmical history; never were the facts discovered, cherished with so true scientific economy; and never was greater industry exhibited in marshaling facts in support of hypotheses and theories.

History is a fascinating study. Nor is the fascination less when we pass from the history of nations and individuals to the history of things. What inquiry could be more absorbing than that into the *origin* of sun, and planets, and moons?

The history of the universe must be gathered, if gathered at all, through scientific research, from the observed condition of those parts of it which are accessible to observation.

Could we determine with certainty the actual condition of the sun, the planets nearest the sun, the planets farthest from the sun, the moons, the comets, the fixed stars, and the *nebulæ;* could we have a record of these conditions at times far remote from each other; could we know what changes have taken place in them within given periods; could we detect an order of causation in these changes, we should have the data for the construction of a cosmical history.

But learned men believe, that with far *less* data than these such a history is possible. Professor Winchell, after referring to the planetary phenomena, says: "This uniformity of conditions, this unanimous obedience to one code of physical laws, implies that all these bodies are urged onward through a common history, and have probably had their starting-point in one common state of matter."

Certainly it would seem highly probable that these bodies have had a common history. Each has, it is true, its own separate individuality. But they are kindred bodies, mutually affecting and being affected by each other.

They are one great family, under one benign government. So related and so balanced are they that we can scarcely conceive that a portion of them could ever have existed without the rest.

They may be composed, in a great degree, of the same kinds of matter, or they may greatly differ.

As to the present condition of their matter, we know that it is not the same in the sun and in the planets.

On the earth we behold continents and oceans, mountains and valleys, and an atmosphere; all adapted to render it a fitting residence for man and other forms of life. Here we witness the phenomenon of combustion. We also witness the production of heat by other chemical combinations and by mechanical and other agencies.

We see the effect of heat on the metals, rendering them incandescent, and even sublimating them. We are also familiar with some of the grand manifestations of heat energy in the earthquake and the volcano. A molten earth, inclosed within a thin shell, is suggested to our thought by what we see. In our imagination we see the shell removed, and the waves of liquid fire in contact with the gases that are free; and we behold a flaming world—a sun—shining with its own light.

It surely is not a very extravagant fancy that pictures the world's history thus. Men of profound learning have generalized from terrestrial *data*, and have thought their generalizations confirmed by the condition of the sun. Just what the solar condition is they do not know, but all agree that it is at least enveloped in flame, and thus to us it *appears* like a globe of fire.

They have reached a conclusion as to the original condition of matter—not of that matter only which has been incorporated into the planetary bodies—not of that only which is now in the sun—but of *all* matter, of which *all* suns and systems that occupy space are composed—and that conclusion is, that the original condition of matter was that of the *nebulæ; and all stars and all planets have come out of this original condition of matter by the operation of a law of evolution.*

Some call this original matter "fire-mist;" some, "luminous vapor;" some, "world stuff." All recognize it as having a real present exemplification in the *nebulæ*, and the theory which, by it, explains the origin of worlds, is called the *Nebular Theory.*

CHAPTER II.

THE NEBULAR HYPOTHESIS.

Discoveries of nebulæ—Simon Marius—Huygens—Halley—Herschell—Lord Rosse—Kant—Laplace—Winchell—Wells—Schedule of cosmical history.

TWO hundred and sixty-three years ago (1612) Simon Marius discovered, in the girdle of Andromeda, an object of unusual interest. It was neither planet nor star, but a luminous fleck on the clear blue firmament, a patch of fire-mist in the sky. This was the first recorded discovery of a *nebula*.

The great *nebula* in Orion was discovered by Huygens in 1656. The discovery filled him with amazement and wonder. His spirit rose to a pitch of ecstasy as he gazed upon what seemed to him like "an opening in the heavens through which a brighter region beyond was visible."

Halley, in 1716, enumerated six *nebulæ*. He also made a few new discoveries.

But it remained for Sir William Herschell,

with the aid of his great telescope, to extend the catalogue to thousands, and to give a new direction to the world's thought respecting them. With an instrument whose penetrative power was one hundred and ninety-two times that of the naked eye, he found many of the *nebulæ* resolved into clusters of stars.

"The principle made use of in the case of resolved clusters Herschell conceived also applicable, through analogy, to groups not unfolding their individual constituents; and he computed that by his four-feet mirror, a cluster of five thousand stars might be descried as a milky spot, although three hundred thousand times deeper in space than Sirius probably is."—*Nichol.*

For a time Herschell thought that *all nebulæ* might be resolved if they could be examined with telescopes of sufficiently high power. This opinion his subsequent investigations led him to abandon, and he, therefore, classed the *nebulæ* as *resolvable* and *irresolvable.*

The *resolvable*, when examined with a telescope of moderate power, still appeared as simple *nebulæ;* but under a telescope of high power, separated into actual clusters of stars.

The *irresolvable nebulæ* retained their apparent continuity under the highest power that Herschel was able to command.

Lord Rosse's great telescope, with a penetrating power five hundred times as great as that of the naked eye, has resolved some of that class which Herschel denominated irresolvable, but there are others which it is unable to resolve.

Thus, down to the present time, the constant enlargement of the range of telescopic observation has been attended with increasing wonders, without putting to rest the great question of the existence of real *nebulæ* in the heavenly spaces.

But that which the telescope could not do, that wonderful instrument, the spectroscope, is supposed to have done. It has established the fact of the existence of luminous nebular bodies in space.

So early as 1655, Kant had given to the world his speculations concerning the *Theory of the Heavens*, in which he outlined a system which other minds subsequently developed into completeness.

How far Herschel may have been affected by a knowledge of the speculations of Kant we know not, but we know that Herschel's genius was not more inventive than logical. He discovered various characteristics of the *nebulæ*, and he went from the *actual*, which he saw, to the logical hypothetical, which could not be seen. There was in some of the *nebulæ* an appearance like a nucleus, from which, outwardly, the mass seemed to thin out until it faded quite away.

This suggested to his mind the idea of compression or condensation of the mass, and he reasoned that the *nebulæ* might be undergoing a process of gradual condensation into stars or suns.

Laplace, who was contemporary with Herschel, seized the thought and carried it out in wider generalization. He saw, in the discoveries of the great Hanoverian, the basis of a cosmical genealogy. Here was a clew to the formation not only of suns, but also of planets and satellites. Assuming the existence of *nebulæ* of such vast magnitude as to fill spaces equal to or greater than that occupied by the entire solar system, he fancied that system to have been evolved, by the operation of natural forces, out of that nebulous mass.

Notwithstanding the authority of Laplace as a mathematician, astronomers were slow to receive this *Nebular Hypothesis.* Many *nebulæ* had been resolved. Might not *all* be similarly constituted, though our instruments were confessedly too feeble to resolve them?

After all, may not the *nebulæ* exist only in appearance? May it not be the blended light of innumerable stars, situated so nearly in the same line of vision that no telescope can ever separate them, and so distant that their light forms but a haze in the open space?

We live in more favored times. Great and wonderful as are the results of telescopic observation, the results of *Spectrum Analysis* are yet more wonderful.

By the spectroscope, light itself is translated into a language of revelation, and, as Schellen says, "we are indebted to it for being able to say with certainty that luminous *nebulæ* actually exist as isolated bodies in space, and that these bodies are luminous masses of gas."

For the purposes of our present inquiry, therefore, we will consider this question settled. We assume the existence of real *nebulæ* —immense volumes of luminous vapor or gas

—filling spaces as ample as that occupied by the solar system, or even greater spaces than that.

Let us now examine the Nebular Hypothesis a little more in detail.

Having, by assumption, the original cosmical matter existing "at such a temperature as to be in the condition of a vapor of great tenuity, stretching across limits wider than the remotest planet," what have been the processes by which that vapor has been transformed and wrought into our sun and the system of planets that revolve around him?

As we propose to examine the nebular theory in its present phases, we will place it before our readers in the language of its latest expounders and advocates.

Professor *Winchell* enunciates the theory as follows: "The cooling and contracting of this vapor inaugurated a rotation which was inevitably accelerated to such an extent that a peripheral ring was detached which became a planet. The same process continued, and other rings were detached, which became planets in due succession. Similarly the planetary masses detached rings, which became their satellites. Thus all the marvelous uniformities of the solar system are but the progeny of that primitive impulse which originated the grand rotation.

"This doctrine has earned unquestioning acceptance, simply because it accords with all the phenomena; and the Nebular Hypothesis, for similar reasons, is rapidly taking its place among established doctrines. Many late discoveries afford unexpected confirmations; and there are few physicists at the present time who continue to withhold their assent. Occasionally we hear a dissenting voice, but it proceeds almost always from persons who, whatever may be their eminence in theology or letters, have little authority in matters of scientific opinion.

"Many interesting deductions follow from the nebular origin of the solar system. The older planets are those remote from the sun, and the youngest planet is Mercury; while the sun is only the residual portion of the cosmical mass, still maintaining an inconceivably high temperature, simply because so vast a body of matter has not yet had time to cool off. The planetary bodies, similarly, must have attained to stages of refrigeration determined by the joint influence of age and mass.

"It is reasonable to suppose that the older planets are composed of a smaller proportion of the denser elements, since they are formed from peripheral portions of the original fire-mist, while it is likely that the denser portions gathered about the center, and entered to a larger extent into the constitution of later rings. The lower specific gravity of the older planets may be partly attributed to this cause. While Mercury, Venus, and Mars do not vary materially from the density of the Earth, Jupiter, Uranus, and Neptune possess only one fourth of the Earth's density and Saturn but one eighth. This circumstance must have much to do with determining the relative proportions of solid and liquid materials upon the several planets at given temperatures, and is thus connected with their adaptability to serve as abodes of organic life."—*Geology of the Stars.*

David A. Wells, an author of excellent standing among educators, and editor of the "Annual of Scientific Discovery," presents the theory as follows:—

"Modern science presents us with only one

hypothesis which, in a consistent and satisfactory manner, attempts to reveal to us the condition of matter, in what may be called the beginning. The outline of this theory, and the evidence upon which it is based, may be briefly stated as follows:—

"Our solar system, of which the earth is a member, viewed superficially, presents to us the idea of a vast luminous body—the sun—occupying a central position, with a number of smaller, though various-sized, bodies revolving at different distances around it, some of which, in turn, have smaller planets or satellites revolving about them.

"A closer examination, however, makes us acquainted with some very singular peculiarities in the structure of this so-called "solar system." Thus, in the first place, it is a very singular fact that the orbits of the planets are all nearly circular, and that their planes are nearly coincident with (or in the same line with) the plane of the sun's equator.

"Next, it is not less remarkable that the motions of the planets around the sun, and the satellites around the planets, and, finally, that the motions of all—sun, planets, and satellites

—around their axes, should be only in one direction, namely, from west to east; that the periods of revolution grow shorter in the planets and satellites as their distances from their primary grow less; that the sun rotates on its axis in a shorter period than that employed in the revolution of any planet, and that every planet, accompanied by satellites, rotates on its axis in a less time than the period of revolution of any satellite.

"These peculiarities suggested to Laplace, the eminent French astronomer and mathematician, the idea that all the matter of the solar system was once a connected mass, endowed with a uniform motion in one direction.

"He further showed, that while this hypothesis and its deductions explained fully the peculiarities noticed, they were not accounted for by any other supposition; and, also, that had the existing arrangement of the solar system been left to accident, the chances against the occurrence of the present organization would have been as four millions of millions to one.

"Coincident with these investigations was the discovery by astronomers of the existence in space, far removed from our system, of an immense number of objects which, from their foggy, cloudy appearance have been called *nebulæ:* some of vast extent and irregular outline, as that in the sword of Orion, which is visible to the naked eye; others of shape more defined and regular; and others, again, in which small, bright *nuclei*, apparently condensed points, appear here and there over the surface. Ascending higher, as it were, in the scale of progress, we have next clusters of *nuclei* with nebulous matter around them; and then what are called 'nebulous stars,' or luminous spherical objects—bright in the center and dull toward the extremities—existing, however, in every stage of concentration, from stars with ill-defined centers to stars invested with only a slight burr or haziness.

"Upon these facts, mainly, has been built up the so-called Nebular Hypothesis which supposes that the various appearances we have described represent the various conditions which suns, systems, and worlds pass through in their progress of formation; the cloudy *nebulæ* representing matter in its original chaotic condition; the defined *nebulæ*, the first stage of condensation; and nucleeatd *nebulæ*, and the succession of nucleated stars, the more advanced and final stages; just as a child, a boy, a youth, a middle-aged and an old man, indicate the successive periods in the life of a human being. But whatever may be the physical condition of the *nebulæ*, the main features of the theory of Laplace curiously accord with the antecedent condition of our system as deduced from its present peculiarities; and it is accordingly inferred that, in the 'beginning,' our solar system was an immense sphere of nebulous matter, filling all the space now occupied by the system, and extending even to a point far beyond the limits of the orbit of Neptune, a planet whose average distance from the sun is about three billions of miles.

"Assuming the existence of such a *nebula* in the first instance, the general attractive force resident in all matter would gradually cause its particles to approach each other, and thus, from the outset, the nebulous sphere must have commenced condensing and contracting. 'It is, moreover, a well-known law of physics, that when fluid matter (gaseous or liquid) collects toward or meets in a center, it establishes rotary motion. Every-day illustrations of this law may be seen in the whirlpool or whirlwind, or, to use a more humble illustration, in water sinking through the aperture of a funnel. Thus rotation on an axis would commence, at first slow, but become quicker and quicker as the condensation increased.' With the establishment of rotary motion, a tendency in the mass to throw off its outer portions would be generated in consequence of the centrifugal force overpowering the central attraction; and it is accordingly supposed that masses of matter were, in fact, from time to time, torn away from the nebulous sphere, which detached portions afterward continued their courses separate from the main mass, but preserving a similar direction in their motion. Such detached masses, abandoned successively at different stages of the condensation, formed themselves into single planets, or, like the great original sphere, into planets with satellites and rings, until, finally, the principal mass condensed itself into the sun, which still occupies its original position as the center of the system, and as the largest body.

"Simultaneously with the commencement of condensation in the nebulous matter, the force *heat* must have manifested itself, since it is a general law of physics that the condensation or compression of all matter, under all circumstances, evolves heat; and as condensation and refrigeration further progressed, by the radiation of heat into space, other forces, as chemical affinity, cohesion, etc., must have exerted an influence, until at last the constituent materials of our earth and the other planetary bodies passed from a gaseous to a fluid or solid condition, and assumed their present forms and properties."

Again, WINCHELL says: "We know enough of the phases of matter, in the different provinces of space, *to feel certain* that they represent progressive stages in the natural evolution of matter as such. Whether seen in *nebula*, star, sun, planet, or satellite, it is a phase in a common history, the earliest periods of which are as truly a part of the history of our world, as the achievements of Alfred the Great are a part of the history of communities of American birth."

He also furnishes us a "tentative exhibit of the successive stages of world matter," and says that "there is little doubt that its general tenor expresses *a fact* in the aspects of the universe."

He divides the entire history into chapters, which he denominates PHASES, and these phases into STAGES.

The phases are the NEBULAR PHASE, the STELLAR PHASE, and the PLANETARY PHASE.

The NEBULAR PHASE has four successive stages:—

1. The stage of gaseity; 2. The stage of normal nebulosity; 3. The stage of continuous fire-mist; 4. The stage of discontinuous fire-mist.

The first of these stages is supposed to be exemplified by "the faint central portions of the annular *nebulæ;*" the second, by "some of the irresolvable *nebulæ;*" the third, by "some of the irresolvable *nebulæ*" and some stars; and the fourth, by "certain resolvable *nebulæ.*"

The STELLAR PHASE has nine successive stages:—

1. The primary nuclear stage; 2. The secondary nuclear stage; 3. The Sirian stage; 4. The Arcturian stage; 5. The solar stage; 6. The variable stage; 7. The liquid stage; 8. The incrustive stage; 9. The eruptive stage.

The first of these stages is supposed to be exemplified by "the planetary *nebulæ*" and the "nebular stars;" the second, by "certain star clusters and most resolvable *nebulæ;*" the third, by white stars; the fourth, by yellow stars; the fifth, by our sun; the sixth, by variable stars; the seventh, by "some star clusters and resolvable *nebulæ;*" the eighth, by red stars; and the ninth, by temporary stars.

The PLANETARY PHASE has five successive stages:—

1. The Saturnian stage; 2. The Jovian stage; 3. The terrestrial stage; 4. The Martial stage; 5. The lunar stage.

These successive stages are supposed to be exemplified by the present condition of Saturn, Jupiter, Earth, Mars, and the Moon. The first exhibits the ring condition; the second the formation of an "atmosphere around the incrusted nucleus," and the production of the lower forms of life; the third witnesses the "culmination of the organic phase;" the fourth witnesses the "decline of the organic phase," and the fifth witnesses the "extinction of organization" and "final refrigeration."

Laplace, a prince among geometricians, declares that he put forth his nebular hypothesis with diffidence. The disciples of Laplace, while carrying the theory beyond the thought of the great master, enunciate it at once with almost dogmatic positiveness and with the richest ornamentation of rhetoric.

Nothing can exceed the enthusiasm of Winchell, unless it be the inconceivably high temperature of the original world stuff. Nothing can compare with the grandeur of his periods, unless it be the original grand rotation itself.

We shall be pardoned, we trust, if we come to the examination and discussion of this subject without enthusiasm. Should our analysis even seem destitute of warmth; should we betray any lack of appreciation of red-hot phrases, we still trust that cool heads will consent to accompany us while we take this nebular theory in pieces and weigh it in the scales of real science. Huge as it is, it will, we think, submit to analysis and test.

CHAPTER III.

CAUSE OF ROTARY MOTION.

Condensation by gravity—Contraction by cooling—Illustration of the process—The whirlwind and whirlpool—Views of Helmholtz—Sterry Hunt—Tyndall—Herbert Spencer.

IT must have been noticed that in the two outlines of the nebular theory which we have quoted there was one point of disagreement, and it was an essential point. What was the cause of the original rotation of the cosmical mass? One class of advocates of the theory answer, "*The cooling, and consequent contraction, of the mass.*" Another class answer, "*The general attractive force resident in all matter.*"

It may not, at first sight, occur to the reader that these two causes could not co-exist. Why not?

If such a nebular sphere did once exist, must there not have been a resident attractive force? Undoubtedly.

But such an exertion of this force as would result in the condensation of the mass, would also have resulted in the evolution of heat. If, then, the cosmical mass was condensed and contracted by the force of gravity, it could not have been contracted by the process of cooling off.

HELMHOLTZ supposes the "heat of the sun to be maintained by the slow condensation of its mass; a diminution by $\frac{1}{1000}$ of its present diameter being sufficient to maintain the present supply of heat for twenty-one thousand years."

Professor WINCHELL, however, is at issue with this theory of condensation, and consequent evolution, of heat. He remarks that, "We cannot safely assert that every or any nebulous body increases in temperature during any period of its history. It seems more probable that a continuous reduction of temperature is experienced, and that the temperature inherent in the sun at the present time is rather the residuum of the primordial heat than the effect of the condensation of his mass.'

To our present inquiry it is a matter of indifference which of these two theories is accepted. The cosmical mass may be conceived of as being condensed by the operation of the resident attractive force, and heated thereby, or it may be conceived of as at an inconceivably high temperature in the beginning, and as gradually dropping its temperature by the radiation of its heat and thus contracting its volume. *In either case, are we furnished with an account of the origin of rotary motion?*

Rotary motion is the one universal fact in the solar system. Rotary motion, in the solar system, *suggested* the hypothesis of cosmical evolution. Rotary motion is a prime factor in the theory. "All the marvelous uniformities of the solar system are but the progeny of that primitive impulse which originated the grand rotation."

To account for the beginning of rotary motion is, therefore, the first duty of the advocate of the nebular theory.

We have before us two methods of doing this. One makes the rotary motion the effect of the cooling, and consequent contraction, of the mass. The other makes the rotary motion the effect of the condensation of the mass by the force of gravity. If either of these alleged causes existed, was it adequate to the alleged effect? If both co-existed and co-operated, were they both, when combined, adequate to the task?

Let us first examine the theory of gravitative force.

The resident attractive force which is in all matter is known to produce the spherical form.

If, therefore, we conceive of matter existing in the nebulous condition, and in a mass of irregular shape, or in detached, but contiguous, masses, we shall readily conclude that this mass, or these masses, will, by the operation of this force, become one spherical mass. We can also readily conceive of a spherical mass of cosmical matter, the diameter of which shall exceed that of the orbit of the most distant planet.

It may not be amiss, at this point, to look at the magnitude of such a sphere, and consider what the condition of the matter of our solar system must have been if thus expanded.

In round numbers, the mean diameter of the orbit of Neptune is about six thousand millions of miles.

The volume of such a sphere would be

115,041,600,000,000,000,000,000,000 cubic miles, or more than three hundred and forty billions' times the present volume of the sun, which is five hundred times the volume of all the planets combined.

Professor HELMHOLTZ—justly distinguished among physicists—says: "If we calculate the density of the mass of our planetary system, according to the above assumption, for the time when it was a nebulous sphere, which reached to the path of the outmost planet, we should find that *it would require several cubic miles of such matter to weigh a single grain.*"

This, then, is the condition of the cosmical matter, when, according to the theory which we are now examining, the general attractive force, which is resident in it, commences the work of inaugurating a rotation of the mass on an axis. Can it do it?

The paramount force, or, rather, the resultant force, exerted by *all* the atoms of the mass upon any single atom, will be in what direction? Toward the center.

It cannot deviate from the center by so much as a hair's breadth. The force of gravity on all parts of the mass must be exactly centripetal.

But can this centripetal tendency of the particles produce rotary motion?

There is nothing in the nature of the force to lead to such a conclusion. On the contrary, all fluid matter possesses a buoyant power exactly proportioned to its density. If all the matter be of uniform density it will be uniformly buoyant, and, though acted on by gravity, it will remain in a state of rest. But if we suppose the atoms of different elements having different specific gravity to seek the center and to gain it at the expense of the lighter elements, then there must arise only a process analogous to that of sedimentary deposition, the moter effect of which would be insensible.

We might conceive of a central nucleus of liquid or solid matter thus being formed; but inasmuch as the deposit would be uniform on all sides and exactly central to the mass, (the lines of descent being exactly centripetal,) we cannot perceive how this could inaugurate rotary motion.

If the matter be not at a temperature too high to admit of increase by this process of condensation, then, evidently, heat must result. But what force, besides heat, is known that is capable of so attenuating the matter which is known to exist in the solar system as to fill the space required by the nebular theory? Nay, is it known that heat itself is capable of doing it? But, if the matter be thus attenuated by heat, could its condensation take place at all except by cooling? But, admitting that it could, have we found a cause for rotary motion? Not yet.

There is a hypothetical deposition of the denser elements. It goes on equally from all sides, and as the denser elements go down, the lighter elements are lifted toward the surface. This process, we should suppose, would result in the gradual arrangement of the cosmical matter in concentric strata, in regular order from the most dense at the center to the least dense at the surface. Two forces, allowing that the elements were freely intermixed in the beginning, might be supposed to counteract this operation of the resident force of gravity.

The force of cohesion, though feeble in its action upon aeriform matter, still performs important offices in the present state of matter. By it we suppose the water of the deep seas to keep up a supply of air sufficient to sustain the life that exists in the waters; and by it the air is enabled to hold aqueous vapors in suspension. By it the atmosphere itself may be said to keep the due proportions of its gaseous constituents always present, for atmospheric air is not a chemical compound, but a mixture. So, also, we may conceive of this cohesive attraction as interfering, in some degree, with the process of stratification in the aeriform cosmical mass. The chemical force—affinity—would at certain temperatures entirely arrest the supposed process of stratification; but it would only arrest it to substitute one of another kind in its place, namely, a stratification of compound substances.

There seem to be two opposite conditions of the original matter assumed by the two classes of nebular theorists. One represents the matter as inconceivably hot. The other represents the matter as heated by the operation of the attractive force.

Assume the truth of the latter representation; then, so soon as the matter reaches a temperature at which affinity can act, there must be general chemical combination. Assume the truth of the former representation;

then, so soon as the temperature gets down low enough, there must be general chemical combination. In either case there would result condensation by combination.

But such condensation could only be of the particles in contact; and we may conceive of the deposition of compounds almost infinitesimally minute, through substances in which affinity was not yet brought into play.

And still in none of the operations, which we have conceived of as possible, is there any thing, so far as we can see, to produce a rotary motion of the mass. But if we assume that the original matter existed at an inconceivably high temperature, then we must consider the elements as free.

Dr. HUNT remarks: "Of the chemical relations of such intensely heated matter, modern chemistry has made known to us some curious facts, which help to throw light on the constitution and luminosity of the sun. Heat, under ordinary conditions, is favorable to chemical combination, but a higher temperature reverses all affinities. Thus the so-called noble metals, gold, silver, mercury, etc., unite with oxygen and other metals; but these compounds are decomposed by heat, and the pure metals are regenerated.

"A similar reaction was many years since shown by Mr. Grove with regard to water, whose elements—oxygen and hydrogen—when mingled and kindled by a flame, or by the electric spark, unite to form water, which however, at a much higher temperature, is again resolved into its component gases. The recent researches of Henry Sainte Claire Deville and others go far to show that this breaking up of compounds, or dissociation of elements by intense heat, is a principle of universal application." Our cosmical matter, then, while existing at an inconceivably high temperature, is free from the action of chemical affinity.

There is but a single force operating to produce any great change in its structure, and that single force is gravity. And we know that, to this force, *all matter, in all conditions*, is subject.

There is no force contemplated as acting on the cosmical mass from beyond itself to give it a rotary motion. The conditions of the nebular hypothesis forbid this. This cosmical history is a history of evolutions. Causation is all within.

The rotary motion had its origin in some primitive impulse, evolved out of the world matter itself, or resident in it. Tyndall refers all the motions of the universe to the gravitative attraction, saying, "The potential energy of gravitation was the original form of all the energy in the universe." If TYNDALL does not *know* who does? Certainly no affirmation could be more positive. HELMHOLTZ also refers the condensation of the original matter to attraction; but he does *not* refer the beginning of rotary motion to the same force. He says we must *assume* its existence. These are his words: "The general attractive force of all matter must, however, impel these masses to approach each other, and to condense, so that the nebulous sphere becomes incessantly smaller, by which, according to mechanical laws, a motion of rotation originally slow, *and the existence of which must be assumed*, would gradually become quicker and quicker."

We are persuaded that HELMHOLTZ is right—the existence of an original rotation must be *assumed*, and if assumed, then we confess that it cannot be accounted for.

But it is alleged that, "It is a well-known

fact that when fluid matter (gaseous or liquid) collects toward or meets in a center, it establishes rotary motion," and the whirlwind and whirlpool are cited as illustrations of this law. But we see no analogy—not the least—between the conditions which produce either of these phenomena, and the supposed conditions of the cosmical mass, whose rotation is to be accounted for.

The whirlpool exhibits the following incidents: 1. An escape of water through an orifice. 2. A flow of the water in the mass toward the orifice seeking an equilibrium. 3. The downward current of escape, and the reaction of the centripetal currents after impact, give rise to a rotary motion, which continues only so long as the equilibrium is unrestored.

But in the nebular mass we have found a perfect equilibrium already existing. The whole mass is supposed to be aeriform and spherical. All is balanced about the center of gravity.

And the center of gravity is not a vacuum into which the cosmical matter rushes, meeting, reacting, and moving off through some outlet opened for it. If we could conceive of an axial outlet, and an equatorial centripetal flow, we might thus imagine the existence of a condition of things analogous to those in the whirlpool.

But we cannot conceive of such an outlet, for the attractions are all so adjusted that every part of the sphere equally distant *from*, is equally drawn *toward* the center. There is no axis, for there is no rotation.

In the whirlpool there is an escape of the water downward, producing a vortex. In the whirlwind there is an escape of the air upward, producing a vortex. Did the force of gravity ever yet produce a vortex by drawing matter into its own center?

In the whirlpool and whirlwind, were there no such escape of the central matter, there could be no centripetal flow. Whenever the orifice is stopped the centripetal flow ceases and the whirlpool ends.

It is by the escaping current that the centripetal currents are modified as they approach the central point, so that they flow not to it, but around it.

Conceive now, not of a sudden rush of matter to a central void; not of the violent impact of elements seeking an avenue of escape, and moving forward after impact to the place of escape by a modified motion; but of a mass of matter in equilibrium, from every point of which there is a gravitation toward the center. That matter which is at the center is at rest. That which is near the center is at rest. All is at rest.

But the specific gravity of the elements being different, the elements also being dissociated, and therefore free to obey the gravitative force, we *may* conceive of them as parting company, and the denser elements descending slowly toward the center. But if such a movement be imagined, it must be supposed to begin simultaneously every-where and to go on equally on all sides. Then the elements of highest specific gravity which are nearest the center will reach it first and rest.

Two motions there would be, the centripetal motion of the denser atoms, and the radial motion of the lighter atoms.

The gravitation of all toward the center simply increases the density of the central matter, and gives it greater buoyant power so long as it remains fluid.

But we do not see any thing in the supposed conditions to produce rotary motion in the mass. We are obliged, then, to declare the problem of rotary motion unsolved by that form of the nebular theory which refers it to the general attractive force.

But what would be the effect of that evolution of heat which must result from condensation? Perhaps it would cause an expansion of the volume. But what then? The direction of the condensing force is centripetal. The expansion must be radial. But this could not originate rotary motion. We know of no law or principle of matter that explains the origin of rotary motion.

Let us now turn to the consideration of the theory enunciated by WINCHELL, which alleges that the rotary motion was caused by the *cooling,* and consequent *contracting,* of the original cosmical sphere.

It is to be regretted that the advocates of this theory have not entered more largely into the discussion of it. No one condescends to give us the rationale of it. How does the process of cooling and contracting the mass impart to it rotary motion?

The cosmical mass is, according to the theory, at an inconceivably high temperature. The phenomenon of combustion, being a chemical one, is impossible, and the heat of the mass is to be conceived of as inherent, and we do not look for its *cause* any more than we look for the cause of the cosmical matter itself. Its presence in the matter is *assumed*. But, as the resident attractive force would act at the very beginning of its existence, (which must have been at the beginning of the existence of the matter itself,) so also the heat, which was likewise in the matter from the beginning, was an active force, and its law was, as it is now, *radiation*.

Modern science teaches that heat is a form of motion. There is molecular motion, which is heat in the mass. There is an interatomic and inter-stellar ether, whose undulatory motions are radiant heat.

We are, then, to conceive of the cosmical matter in a state of high heat, that is, pervaded throughout with the highest thermal activity, which is imparted to the enveloping ether, and thus radiated into space, its radiations proceeding in right lines, the same as light.

The radiation is from the entire surface. The thermal activity is equal over the entire surface. The ethereal envelope is homogeneous every-where, and therefore the cooling must go on equally over every part of the surface. Moreover, if by convection or otherwise the interior heat be so brought to the surface as to maintain nearly the same temperature throughout the mass, still the cooling will take place equally in all directions from the center.

The cooling of the surface would contract the surface, and the cooling of the mass would contract the mass. But the contraction would be in the direction of the center. It would be equivalent to a subsidence of the surface. Could this insensible universal depression of the surface produce a rotary motion of the mass? We see not how it could.

But it is gravely urged that we have an illustration and proof of this theory, also, in the whirlwind and whirlpool; and we are obliged to re-examine those phenomena, which, if not analogous to the supposed action of the cosmical matter under the influence of gravity, are, we think, no more analogous to the behavior of the cosmical matter under the conditions we are now considering.

The whirlpool, on a small scale, is a familiar object. We observe the displacement of a central body of water, the rush of the external water to the space thus made vacant, and the impact of the currents thus formed.

The momentum of the innumerable centripetal currents at the moment of impact must entirely neutralize those currents, or cause a rebound in the lines in which they approached the center, or they must change their direction. The escaping current determines the result by forming a column of transverse motion. Without arresting the centripetal currents, it changes their direction downward, so that there arises a resultant motion, which is spiral.

Were there no centripetal momentum, or were the orifice of escape so large as to allow of no reactions, there could be no whirlpool. But it should not be forgotten that the rotary motion *begins at the center, or the place of discharge, that it tends to produce a vortex, and that it enlarges its circles outwardly.*

It does not begin on the exterior, and communicate its motion inwardly till the whole mass is in motion. But is not this what the theory of *cooling and contracting* assumes? The assumption is contrary to the phenomena cited to support it.

But it may be asked, "How did the rotary motion originate? There is rotary motion. How do you account for it?"

We do not account for it. We have no physical theory on the subject.

Mr. Herbert Spencer exhibits the *rationale* of axial rotation as follows: "If we assume the first stage in nebular condensation to be the precipitation into floculi of denser matter previously diffused through a rarer medium, (a supposition both physically justified and in harmony with certain astronomical observations,) we shall find that nebular motion is interpretable in pursuance of the above general laws. Each portion of such vapor-like matter must begin to move toward the common center of gravity. The tractive forces, which would of themselves carry it in a straight line to the center of gravity, are opposed by the resistant forces of the medium through which it is drawn.

"The direction of movement must be the resultant of these—a resultant which, in consequence of the unsymmetrical form of the floculus, must be a curve directed not to the center of gravity but toward one side of it. And it may be readily shown, that, in an aggregation of such floculi severally thus moving, there must, by composition of forces, eventually result a rotation of the whole *nebula* in one direction."

But does not Mr. Spencer in this instance, and in other instances in which he substantially repeats these thoughts, totally ignore one of the established principles of natural philosophy, namely, the equality of action and reaction? Supposing it to be true that the descending floculi are unsymmetrical, and that their unsymmetrical forms are all exactly alike, and that their corresponding parts were set in the directions must favorable for giving to them severally that exact direction which would result in *their* reaching, not the *center* of gravity, but a *line* which would be the axis of their combined motion, would it follow that the *whole nebula* would take such an axial motion?

What becomes of that *resisting* medium

through which the floculi descend? How does it cease to be a resisting medium? The degree of force with which it resists is supposed to be sufficient to divert the floculi from their perpendicular descent. But the resisting medium can exert no more resistant force than the descending floculi exert of *direct* force. Then the *medium* must have a motion imparted to it. And *its* motion must be exactly opposite to that of the floculi. If the floculi descend in curves, the medium will ascend in opposite curves. No axial rotation of the whole mass can arise here until there be a suspension of the law that action and reaction are equal. If, then, "We *assume* the first stage in nebular condensation," we are *not* able to interpret the axial motions of worlds by that assumption. We are obliged also to *assume* that the nebular mass had an original rotary motion, for the beginning of which modern science is unable to account, just as it is unable to account for the nebular matter itself.

CHAPTER IV.

RING FORMATIONS.

Rings of Saturn—Plateau's experiment—The centrifugal force—Discussion of principles—The sphere—The spheroid—Calculations of oblateness—Could rings be detached?

ASSUMING the existence of the nebulous cosmical sphere; assuming that it has in some way received a rotary motion; assuming that it cooled and contracted, and that its rotary motion was accelerated; we now come to the examination of the next chapter of the cosmical history.

What has the rotary motion accomplished? The Nebular Hypothesis tells us what:—

"A peripheral ring was detached which became a planet. The same process continued and other rings were detached, which became the other planets in due succession. Similarly, the planetary masses detached rings which became their satellites. Thus all the marvelous uniformities of the solar system are but the progeny of that primitive impulse which originated the grand rotation."—*Winchell.* "A peripheral ring" is certainly a pleasant euphony. A "primitive impulse, which originated the grand rotation," is a truly sonorous phrase.

But it is not unreasonable to ask, Have we any warrant in known principles and facts to justify the conception which these terms express?

The advocates of the Nebular Hypothesis refer us to the revelations of the telescope. There is, it is alleged, an instance of the ring-condition to be seen in the heavens. Saturn has rings. It is conjectured that Neptune has rings. "In Saturn we discover a planet which, if we may trust the determinations, is even lighter than water. No surface features of the body are discernible, and it seems, like Jupiter, to remain enveloped in a mass of belted clouds. Its most striking phenomena are its eight satellites and its grand system of rings.

"*The first thought suggested by the latter is their demonstration of the truth of the nebular theory of planetary origin. Here we have, as a fact, a perpetual instance of the ring condition—a demonstration even more convincing than the laboratory experiment of Plateau. Is this* planet in a more primitive condition than Jupiter, at once the younger and the larger body?

"An affirmative answer is indicated both by the rings and the low specific gravity; and the intensity of its light, making allowance for greater distance and inferior bulk, is almost equal to that of Jupiter.

"But the substance of the rings is not aeriform, as we suppose the normal ring-condition to be. It is neither solid nor fluid, as Professor Pierce has demonstrated; but, according to a suggestion of Proctor, may be in a granular state—each constituent grain (so to speak) answering to a miniature moon, and the whole assemblage, millions in number, disposing themselves, according to the varying influences, in two, three, or more annuli."—*Winchell.*

This seems to us a singular medley of strangely contradictory statements. First. In Saturn we have, "*as a fact,* a perpetual instance of the ring-condition;" but afterward there is no ring-condition at all, but millions of miniature moons. Secondly. This "perpetual instance of the ring-condition" (which, after all, is *not* an instance of the ring condition) is a "demonstration of the truth of the nebular theory of planetary origin;" and yet, though according to that theory the ring-condition is an *aeriform* condition, this system of miniature moons is *not* a system of aeriform bodies. Instead, then, of being a demonstration of the truth of the nebular theory of planetary origin, it is suggestive of the incompatibility of that theory with the observed facts of planetary existence. The non-continuity of the apparent rings, which has been suggested by Proctor, is now generally received as a truth by astronomers, who are able only on this supposition to account for their observed motions.

Nor is it difficult to understand how *less than millions* of small moons, revolving around the body of Saturn in orbits whose planes lie edgewise, or slightly inclined to our line of vision, and completing their revolution in ten hours and thirty-two minutes, should produce the illusion of a ring-condition. A few hundred small moons flying at the rate of 48,000 miles an hour would, we think, be sufficient to produce the illusion. Yet it is no more incredible that thousands of moons should be found revolving around a planet, than that thousands of asteroids should be revolving around the sun inside the orbit of Jupiter.

The laboratory experiment of Plateau is also referred to. This experiment has been the ground of a vast amount of faith in the nebular theory. Winchell says, it is convincing; but the ring-condition of Saturn is *demonstration*, more convincing. Our readers will, therefore, give to Plateau's celebrated experiment the consideration it deserves.

Certainly, we must admit that the first announcement of the experiment produced a great sensation in scientific circles.

M. Plateau, a Belgian physicist, succeeded in producing rings around a revolving body.

If any one wishes to try the experiment let him take a glass vessel and fill it half full of spirits of wine. Now drop into it a small quantity of olive oil. The oil, being of greater specific gravity than the spirits, will sink. Now add water until the specific gravity of the mixture is just sufficient to float the oil *near* the surface. The oil will have assumed the globular form. Now, through the globule of oil pass a wire, which has first been mechanically adjusted so that it can be rapidly revolved. Revolve it, at first slowly, then gradually increase the rapidity of the rotation. The oil globe will revolve around the wire as an axis. With the increase of the velocity of rotation the globe flattens, and finally detaches a ring, which breaks up into globules, and they revolve around the central portion. This is the experiment which is only less convincing as to the truth of the nebular theory of planetary origin than the demonstration afforded by the ring-condition of Saturn; a condition which, it is confessed, does not exist at all.

Let us now examine this experiment. What are the elements of it which are analogous to the details of the nebular theory, so that *this* is worthy to convince an intelligent inquirer of the truth of *that?*

1. The substance chosen for the experiment is one which has a high degree of coherency compared with its specific gravity. The cosmical mass is supposed to have been aeriform, and of extreme tenuity, in which case its coherency must have been almost zero.

2. The attractions of the particles of the oil for each other are so feeble that they are only

able to produce the spherical arrangement when inclosed in a medium of the same specific gravity, and, when revolved, they the more readily obey the centrifugal force, and the whole mass breaks up into fragments; but the masses which are supposed to have been *detached* from the cosmical sphere were minute portions compared to the whole mass which remained unbroken.

3. The experimental substance revolves by the application of external force; but the cosmical sphere is supposed to have revolved by a force originating within itself.

4. The experimental substance revolved in a medium of its own specific gravity. But the cosmical sphere is supposed to have revolved in void space.

5. The experimental substance is subject to the frictional resistance of the medium in which it revolves, which resistance must increase as the revolving substance flattens and extends. But the cosmical sphere is not supposed to have been thus resisted by any external matter.

6. The rotation of the oil globule imparts to the medium in which it floats a rotary

motion. The centrifugal force having overcome the coherency of the oil, it breaks up into minuter globules, and these continue to revolve for a time, being carried around by the circular current of the medium itself. But the detached masses of nebulous matter are not supposed to have floated in any medium whose motion directed theirs.

Are the *physical conditions in the two cases the same or analogous?*

Are the motor forces the same or analogous?

Are the results the same or analogous?

To each of these questions we think the unbiased mind will answer no.

The *fact* that the globule of oil is flattened and enlarged and broken up into minuter globules, and revolved around the center, is the only feature of the experiment which may be said to be analogous to the assumptions of the nebular theory; and here the analogy is only phenomenal.

Could M. Plateau devise some means by which a globe of air could be revolved in a void, and air rings could be detached by the centrifugal force alone, and these rings could be gathered into smaller air globes and kept revolving around the parent mass in the void, he would thus exhibit something more nearly analogous to the hypothetical cosmical evolution.

Having thus glanced at the supposed illustrations and demonstrations of the nebular theory, afforded on the grand scale by the phenomenal ring-condition of Saturn, and on the minute scale by a few drops of oil, we now wish to examine the theory on its own premises, and bring it to the test of philosophical and mathematical principles.

For this purpose we assume the existence of the spherical cosmical mass in space uninfluenced by any force outside of itself, and we assume for this spherical mass an axial rotation, which by the contraction of the mass must have been accelerated. So much we assume with the advocates of the theory.

Now we know that rotary motion produces what is known as the centrifugal force. But the centrifugal force is nothing more or less than the tendency of a body moving in a circle to go on exactly in the direction in which it is moving at any given point in the circle, and that direction is always a tangent of the circle.

The centrifugal force is the projectile force of circular motion.

With the increase of the rate of rotation there is an increase of this projectile force. If we double the rate of motion we quadruple the force of the same mass. But whatever may be the rate of the rotation, a projectile can never be thrown farther out by the centrifugal force than the tangent of the circle. Conceive now of every point on the circle as being thus projected along the tangent line, and the result must be an expansion of the circle itself to an extent determined by the rate of motion.

But the rate of rotation being the same in circles of different diameters, that is, the complete revolution being accomplished in the same time, the larger the circle the greater the centrifugal force, because the velocity must be greater.

If, then, a sphere be rotating on its axis, its greatest circle of rotation will be its equator; and every parallel of latitude will be a smaller circle of rotation, until at the pole it will be, so to speak, the rotation of a point. Therefore, at the poles there can be no centrifugal force, while at every successive point, in passing from the pole to the equator, there will be an increasing centrifugal force, and at the equator the greatest of all. If, then, the substance of the revolving sphere be of a yielding nature, the effect of the centrifugal force must be to elevate the equatorial region, and, correspondingly, to depress the polar region.

We have an example of the effect of the centrifugal force on the shape of a revolving sphere in the earth itself. Here the equatorial region has been elevated and the polar region depressed until there is a difference of twenty-six and a half miles between the polar diameter and the equatorial diameter.

By the centrifugal force the earth is rendered an oblate spheroid.

To indicate the *rate* of the rotary motion in different bodies we notice the time of the rotation, and what part of a complete rotation is performed in a certain specified time.

Usually one hour is the specified unit of time. Then, inasmuch as the earth revolves on its axis once in twenty-four hours, it must perform one twenty-fourth of a revolution in one hour. But $\frac{1}{24}$ of a rotation is $\frac{1}{24}$ of 360 degrees, or fifteen degrees; and, therefore, we say that the rate of the earth's axial rotation is fifteen degrees an hour, just as we would say of a railroad train that it moves at the rate of fifteen miles an hour.

Miles are a definite linear measure. Degrees are a definite circular measure; but it must be remembered that the rate is the same for all parallel circles of the same sphere, be they great or small.

The earth's axial rotation at the rate of fifteen degrees an hour produces a centrifugal force sufficient to make the equatorial diameter twenty-six and a half miles greater than the polar diameter; making the oblateness of the earth $\frac{1}{260}$ of its mean diameter.

The planet Jupiter affords a still more striking example of the effect of the centrifugal force in giving oblateness to a spheroid. The axial rotation of Jupiter is accomplished in less than ten hours.

The rate of the rotation is, therefore, thirty-six degrees per hour, which is two and two fifths times that of the earth. Moreover, the density of Jupiter is only about one fourth that of the earth, and hence, by estimation, the oblateness of Jupiter has been found to be about $\frac{1}{13}$ of his mean diameter, but by observation it is $\frac{1}{17}$.

Saturn is a still more remarkable example, his oblateness being about $\frac{1}{10}$ of his diameter. The axial rotation is at a lower rate than that of Jupiter, but its density is also only about half as great. Great, however, as is the oblateness of Saturn, a person standing on its equator would have around him an expanse the curvature of whose surface would be much less than that of the earth's equatorial region.

What would be the effect were the axial rotation of Jupiter to be accelerated to twice its present rate?

Then its rate would be seventy-two degrees an hour, or 4.8 times as great as that of the earth. The centrifugal force of this high rate of rotation would be about twenty-three times that of the earth's rotation if the two bodies were of equal density; but as Jupiter's density is only one fourth that of the earth, the effect of centrifugal force will be four times as great, and will be expressed by $\frac{92}{200}$ of the diameter; for $4.8^2 \times 4 \times \frac{1}{200} = \frac{92}{200}$. The oblateness of Jupiter would then be one third of his mean diameter. And yet Jupiter would be but a spheroid.

So far as we can see, in the light of known physical principles, the continuity of the planetary substance would remain unbroken. The polar diameter would still be fifty-six thousand miles, and its meridional curvature at the equator would be far less than that of the earth at the present time.

We can see no promise here of ring formations.

Apply the same principles to the supposed original cosmical mass, a sphere more than six thousand millions of miles in diameter. Imagine it in motion on an axis. Imagine it extending out equatorially and settling down at the poles; to what extent can this process be carried, and what will result?

Is the rotary motion, however much it may be accelerated, adequate to the production of a peripheral ring?

We must not forget that this cosmical sphere is revolving in a void. There is no external matter whose friction or attraction can modify the result. If it be alleged that there is other matter in the universe whose attraction must have reached the cosmical sphere and affected it, we reply that the nebular hypothesis does not take such external attractions into account. It professes to find all its world-forming forces within the mass, and the whole planetary history is one of *evolution*.

The only force accredited with the work of producing a peripheral ring is the centrifugal force. The ring is only alleged as an incident in the process of planetary genesis by the grand rotation, and the ring is alleged only because the centrifugal force is known to enlarge the equatorial measure of a sphere.

The force of gravity would arrange the cosmical matter into a true sphere. The centrifugal force would change it into a spheroid. But the equation of these two forces will always be such that there cannot be such a thing as the casting off of any portion of the mass. We could conceive of the entire cosmical matter as assuming the form of a ring, but we know of no fact in nature, and no principle, that warrants the idea that a ring could be detached.

But we may readily conceive that another effect, which also is claimed by the advocates of the nebular theory, would follow. The more elongated the spheroid became the more extensive would be the surface exposed to the outlying frigid space, and the more rapidly the mass must cool off and contract. If we suppose the equatorial region to be thinnest it must contract most rapidly, and by its contraction diminish the oblateness of the spheroid.

The advocates of the theory find, in this equatorial contraction, the means of accelerating the rotary motion. And yet none of them have appeared to be conscious that *an elongation of the equatorial diameter must, on the same rational grounds, diminish the rate of the rotary motion.* But if the contraction of the circle of rotation accelerates the velocity, the enlargement of the circle of rotation must diminish the velocity.

Here, then, in the nebular theory, we have dilation and contraction hypothetically incident to the cosmical history, incidents alleged by the theory, and one of them quoted to show how the grand rotation was "inevitably accelerated;" the other quoted only to show how the ring-condition could arise, quite unconscious of the truth that, if contraction accelerates, dilation must retard, the rotary motion. Between them must not the rotary motion remain constant?

But, in any event, we do not find that the centrifugal force could detach a ring from the equatorial regions of the mass. The centrifugal force acting proportionately at all latitudes, the thinning out at the equator cannot be such as would be required to meet the exigencies of the theory. *The whole figure must be proportionately molded by the forces which are at work.*

As the equator arises the pole must be depressed, and every point between them must be affected. Not to the extent to which the equatorial matter is projected outward by the centrifugal force, but to an extent proportionate to the diameters of the circles, will the matter under every parallel of latitude be projected forward by the centrifugal force in the planes of those circles, while the gravity of all will tend toward the center of the mass.

Thus, while the centrifugal force would flatten the spheroid, the gravity of the mass binds it, as nearly as possible, to the spherical form.

Gravitation assures the continuity of the mass.

In Plateau's experiment the only binding force was the cohesive attractions of the molecules of oil. Cohesive attraction once overcome, either by the centrifugal force or by abrasion by the medium in which the matter revolved, the oil globules could only separate; and the rotation of the medium continuing, the globules could only continue on, borne by the circular currents around the axis of rotation. But gravitation is never overcome. It continues to act on the mass and on each atom of the mass through all distances and in all situations, and so it binds the mass together.

We can, as before stated, conceive of a rotation which would throw all the matter of a sphere out from the center, so that the sphere would become a ring; but the ring would be cylindrical, and there is nothing in the single fact of rotation to shatter such a ring into fragments so long as its constituent materials remain plastic. But the formation of such a ring is not in the Nebular Hypothesis.

Moreover, the supposition that such a ring could be produced by such a rotary motion as would arise from *inevitable* acceleration, is opposed by the postulate that it is contraction which accelerates the rotary motion, for by our supposition there is not contraction but diametrical enlargement of the revolving mass.

The nebular theory, however, does not contemplate the formation of such a ring. The ring hypothetical is a peripheral ring. We are to conceive of the cosmical spheroid as letting go of its equatorial protuberance, so that it became detached, lifted away from the body of the spheroid, and left to revolve on its own account. But the advocates of the theory do not explain by what force the matter which is thus separated is lifted away, while the adjacent matter is not lifted away. No repulsions enter into this theory.

The "grand rotation" accounts for everything.

But we submit that, according to the theory, the grand rotation involves the whole mass of the cosmical matter.

There is a rotation of the earth, and it elevates the equatorial region, but it does not lift it away from the earth, and it never did. That the "moon is an outlying fragment of the earth's former equator," may be an allowable figure of speech, but it is a bald assumption in physics.

The truth is, that just so soon as there is an elevation of the equatorial surface, the force of gravity brings in supporting matter from the latitudes, and the continuity is maintained.

And it must be so always, unless there be some adverse principle of physics of which we are not yet informed.

CHAPTER V.

ACTUAL VELOCITIES.

Actual velocities—The Sun's motions—Planetary motion—
"The original grand rotation."

HAVING considered the possible effects of a supposed accelerated velocity in the rotation of the cosmical mass, we now come to the consideration of actual velocities.

Taking a survey of the solar system, we find that rotary motion exists in two forms, which we denominate *axial* and *orbital*.

The axial rotation is the rotation of a body on its own axis. Such a rotation is found in the sun, in most of the planets, and in their satellites. Uranus and Neptune are not positively known to revolve on their axes, but the analogies of the system justify the belief that they do.

Orbital motion is the motion which one body has while revolving around another body.

The satellites revolve in orbits around the planets of which they are the satellites. The planets revolve, in orbits, around the sun, carrying their satellites with them.

The asteroids are small planets which revolve also around the sun.

Besides these examples of rotary motion, that granular system, which was long regarded as a system of rings, revolves around the planet Saturn in nearly circular orbits. The comets, also, because they revolve around the sun, are to be considered as belonging to the solar system; yet, because of the great eccentricity of their orbits and the great length of their periodic times, are regarded as strangers and foreigners. Still the comets must be accounted for as members of the cosmical family.

The sun itself is moving through the heavens in the direction of the constellation Hercules, according to Herschell. Herschell announced his discovery in 1783, fixing the point in the heavens toward which the sun is moving at two hundred and fifty-seven degrees in right ascension and twenty-five degrees northern declination.

MAEDLER has announced, as the result of his observations and estimates, that the center of the sun's orbit is in the neighborhood of Alcyone. Although no one, so far as we know, has computed all the elements thereof, there is little reason to doubt that the sun revolves in an orbit. And this fact carries our thought to another beginning. Cosmical history is but meager if it leave out the origin of the solar cosmical mass itself. If satellites are the progeny of the rotation of planetary masses—if planets are the progeny of the rotation of that cosmical mass of which the sun is the residuum—then, whence this vast cosmical mass itself, which originally embraced not only the sun, but also all the planets and all the satellites? Was it also once a peripheral ring? If so, of what? And has the sun an orbital motion through space which is the progeny of a still older and grander rotation?

But let us return. We are ascending heights, whence, looking down, thought grows dizzy.

If the Nebular Hypothesis be true, we ought to be able to find some trace of the "original grand rotation." Somewhere, among all these revolving bodies, there must be at least a clew to it.

The theory is, that the original cosmical

sphere in some way obtained an axial rotation. This axial rotation was accelerated to such a degree that it cast off from the original a planetary mass, which continued to revolve around the parent body. Though the motion of the original mass was axial, yet the continued motion of the planetary mass was orbital, and it also acquired an axial motion.

The original mass is supposed to have gradually contracted; its motion was thereby accelerated, and it threw off another planetary mass. The first planetary mass also contracted, its axial motion was accelerated, and it threw off a mass which became a satellite. And this process continued until all the planets were thrown off from the original, and all the satellites from their planets.

Such is the theory, and in the light of it we again remark, we surely ought to be able to find a clew to the original grand rotation.

We suppose, in fact, that *the orbital velocity of each of the planets must indicate what the axial velocity of the cosmical mass was at the time that each planetary mass was projected into space.*

No one will, we think, claim that the velocity of the planetary mass in its orbit could be greater than the axial velocity which projected it into space.

Allowing that it received a certain initial velocity at the moment of detachment, it would maintain that velocity only until the attraction of the parent mass should overcome it, and it would then commence a return toward its source. After commencing its return its velocity must be accelerated until its centrifugal force should again preponderate and carry it away into remoter space again. *But the mean of its velocities would be its original velocity, and its orbital period would be the time occupied by the parent mass in making one axial revolution at the date when the planetary mass was detached.*

The next question which arises is this: Is the orbital period of a planet *now* what it was when the planetary mass was detached?

We know of no force but gravity to affect planetary motion; and we have seen what the result would be when there was but a single planetary mass and the original cosmical mass within the limits of the solar system.

When other planetary masses were detached,

the relative positions of these masses would temporarily affect the result. But there could never arise such a collocation of the spheres as would destroy the equilibrium of the system as a whole. Suppose, then, that the orbital motion of one planetary mass be at one time so retarded by the attraction of another planetary mass as to lengthen its periodic time, at another time the effect of the attraction of the same planetary mass will be to shorten its periodic time, so that the sum of all its effects shall be zero. Then the periodic times may be said to be the same from age to age.

The mathematics of astronomy are exceedingly exact. The planetary periods are computed to seconds of time. And so reliable are these computations, that on the credit of them individuals, learned societies, and even nations, incur vast expense and fit out expeditions for the purpose of observing certain astronomical phenomena which have been predicted for years. They are predicted mathematically. The very second when the phenomenon shall be first visible, and the spot on the earth's surface from which, if atmospheric conditions are favorable, it can be most advantageously observed, are noted and announced.

We write in December, 1873, and yet we know that on the 8th of December, 1874, a transit of Venus will occur. But we know, also, that if we would see it we must have a station somewhere in the remote east; for only to Asia, Australia, the Sandwich Islands, etc., will it be visible. Already the world is astir with preparations to observe that transit. The world has faith in astronomical calculations. It is entirely within the range of such computations to declare the exact moment of the beginning of an eclipse of the sun a thousand years hence, and to describe its character, as partial, total, or annular, and to announce to what portions of the earth it will be visible. In like manner astronomers foretell the time of a conjunction of any two of the planets, or of any planet with the sun, or the occultation of planet or fixed star.

True, all this would be possible were the orbital periods variable quantities, provided the increment of variation were known. But so far as we know there is no permanent change in the orbital periods.

It is true that we do not find *uniform* orbital motion. The orbits are all more or less elliptical, and the planets move from their aphelion to their perihelion with accelerated velocity, and from their perihelion to their aphelion with retarded velocity. But while the motion is thus variable, the mean of their motions for a thousand years is a constant quantity.

The *axial* periods, or planetary days, are unchanging. Here we find what we do not find in the orbital motion, absolutely unvarying *rate* of motion.

Of orbital motion we speak of the perihelion velocity, the aphelion velocity, and the mean velocity. But when we speak of the axial rotation of a planet we never speak of different velocities.

The rate of rotation is constant—unvarying. From day to day, from year to year, from age to age, it changes not. It is the *one only* uniform motion of which we know any thing. What the axial rotation of the earth was at the morning of time, that it is now. "The earth has not varied in its revolution," says Steele, "$\frac{1}{100}$ of a second in 2,000 years." Then it does not vary a second in two hundred thousand years. Laplace estimated the variation at $\frac{1}{300}$ of a second in 2,000 years, which would be at the rate of one second in 600,000 years.

Such being the constant character of planetary periods, we are justified in the declaration that the present orbital period of *each planet* must indicate what the *axial* period of the cosmical mass was at the time the planetary mass was detached. And if this conclusion is justified, then the axial period of the "original grand rotation" was exactly what the orbital period of Neptune now is.

And, indeed, we understand the advocates of the nebular theory to affirm substantially the same thing. They reason from the *present motions* of the solar system. The planets *now* revolve on their axes; the sun *now* revolves on its axis; the planets and their satellites *now* revolve in orbits, the planetary orbits are *now* nearly circular, and they are *now* nearly in one plane, etc. These are facts which are now observable in the mechanism and movements of the planetary system, and they are supposed to point to a condition of the planetary matter and to movements therein millions of ages ago.

In maintaining, therefore, the postulate that the axial period of the original cosmical mass *was* what the orbital period of Neptune *is*, we think we are supported by the reasoning of the nebular theorists themselves.

Now we propose to examine the orbital period of Neptune with the view of ascertaining *what was the original grand rotation.* When we have found it we will examine it for the purpose of determining the question of its adequacy to produce a peripheral ring, supposing the production of such a ring to be possible under any circumstances.

The sidereal period of Neptune is 60,127 days or 1,443,048 hours. The *rate* of the rotation, then, is, .00025 of a degree (twenty-five, one hundred thousandths of one degree) per hour, or about $\frac{1}{11}$ of a second per hour. The rate of the earth's rotation is fifteen degrees an hour, and at this rate it produces an oblateness of only $\frac{1}{315}$. But this rate is sixty thousand times as great as that of the supposed cosmical mass, and on matter of the specific gravity of water would be six hundred million times as efficient in producing oblateness as the rate of motion found in the original grand rotation.

The conclusion we reach is this—the ascertained rate of the supposed cosmical rotation is totally inadequate to produce a very considerable oblateness of the cosmical sphere.

It is not our purpose to indulge in extended mathematical calculations, but it will not be deemed amiss to refer to some of the data to be considered.

Notice, first, the immensity of the supposed cosmical sphere. Its great circle is about six thousand millions of miles in diameter.

How small an angle does the tangent of this vast circle form with the circle itself. Yet the centrifugal force can project the peripheral matter only along the tangent.

The velocity of projection at each initial point is 12,000 miles an hour. The arc of the circle passed over in an hour is, as we have seen, only one eleventh of a second. It will, therefore, require the equivalent of a projection continued for one hour to lift the surface outward to the measure of the tangent of an arc of one eleventh of a second, and this, too, without considering the effect of gravity on the projected mass.

Is it too much to ask of the advocates of the nebular theory to estimate the force of gravity on the surface of the hypothetical cosmical sphere, and the exact elevation that *could* be given to the equatorial region by the centrifugal force?

Is it not, indeed, their duty to do this, and thus demonstrate the adequacy of the centrifugal force to produce the effects ascribed to it by the theory?

Do they answer, "We have not the exact data necessary to an estimate? We do not know the exact magnitude of the original cosmical mass at the time of detaching the planetary mass? We do not know its rate of motion? We do not know the gravitative force of the original mass?"

Indeed! Do you not know these things? Do you assume every thing? Is every thing to be taken for granted? And is that science? Well, whatever you may hereafter do in behalf of the theory, will you show us that a rotation at the rate of .00025 of a degree per hour is sufficient to produce even a great degree of oblateness in such a body as the original cosmical mass is supposed to have been? When you do that, it will be time to extend the inquiry to the possibility of detaching a peripheral ring by the same velocity

Let us dismiss Neptune and glance at the actual velocities of the other planets.

The following table shows the mean rate per hour of the orbital motion of each of the planets named: URANUS, .00049 of a degree; SATURN, .0014 of a degree; JUPITER, .0034 of a degree; MARS, .021 of a degree; EARTH, .041 of a degree; VENUS, .066 of a degree; MERCURY, .17 of a degree.

The sun's axial rotation at the rate of .6 of a degree per hour produces no perceptible oblateness. Suppose the sun to be expanded to the dimensions of the orbit of Mercury and to embrace that planet, meanwhile dropping his rate of axial rotation until it should coincide with the orbital rate of Mercury, (.17 of a degree,) would it then exhibit any perceptible oblateness?

CHAPTER VI.

DIRECTION OF PLANETARY MOTIONS.

Laws of centrifugal projection—In what direction must the planet be moving?—Where is the plane of original rotation?—The sun's rotation—Inclination of planetary orbits to the sun's equatorial plane—Comets—Asteroids—Satellites—Ratio of the axial rotation to the orbital.

IN the preceding chapter we considered the actual velocities of the planetary system, and we arrived at the conclusion that the velocities with which the planets revolve in their respective orbits are not adequate to the production of the peripheral rings contemplated by the Nebular Hypothesis, and that, therefore, these velocities are not such as to *account for the origin* of the planets on the principles of that hypothesis.

But the advocates of the hypothesis also allege that the *direction* of the planetary motions and of the axial motion of the sun point to the same rational conclusion, the truth of the nebular theory. Thus says Winchell:

"Each has continued in an orbit which marks the periphery of the parent mass at the time of the planet's separation. All continue to revolve in the same direction as the parent mass and the resultant sun. All revolve in very nearly the plane *which must always have been the plane of the equator of the mass*—the astronomical ecliptic. All continue to revolve upon their own axes, in the same direction as required by the motion of the parent mass. Can all these be so by chance? Can these planetary movements thus correspond, and the material constitution of all these bodies be identical, without leaving a profound conviction upon our minds that they have had a common origin and a common history?"

The foregoing illustrates how differently men will reason from the same premises. With Winchell, the alternative of admitting that the planetary motions indicate an origin of worlds in the development plan, is the supposition that the planetary system is a *chance system*. But another man, looking at the same system, would conclude that the happy adjustments of the system simply indicate *design*, and the direct and immediate agency of a superintending *intelligence;* and he would no more think of a *natural development* of worlds out of fire-mist than he would think of chance. In fact he would think of both suppositions as equally irrational.

But in the inquiry we are now pursuing we exclude all reasoning of this kind. To the results we seek, it is all one whether the solar system proclaims the existence of an infinite intelligence—the Creator and upholder of all things—or not. Our subject is a material subject. The worlds are material worlds. The only *forces* of which we take account are the forces which are known as material forces, or the forces which inhere in matter and which operate according to fixed laws. Whether these forces, and the laws according to which they act, and the matter on which they act, each or all are the offspring of chance or the offspring of intelligence, is, therefore, of no account in our estimation.

We take this planetary structure as it is, we consider its material elements, and the laws which are known to govern them just as they are, and, by the *facts which we find existing*, we try the Nebular Hypothesis.

Our next examination will be of the *laws of centrifugal projection*.

A mass of matter revolving on an axis always generates what is called centrifugal force. If any portion of the mass is free to leave the other portions of the mass, it will be thrown off. If all portions of the mass are equally free to obey the impulse of the centrifugal force, all parts will move outwardly with a force determined by the relative situation of the parts. But there is one *law* of centrifugal projection which is of so great importance to our inquiry that we wish to give it in form as follows: THE PROJECTILE ALWAYS MOVES IN A DIRECTION AT RIGHT ANGLES WITH THE AXIS OF ROTATION.

Now we demand that when a theory accounts for the formation of worlds by centrifugal projection, the theory shall be supported by this *law* of centrifugal projection. Let us assume, with the theory, that this force did detach peripheral rings, that these rings did become planets, and that "each has continued to revolve in an orbit which marks the periphery of the parent mass at the time of planet's separation," then in what direction should we expect to find planets *now* moving?

Is not the answer evident? *What is the law? The direction of the projection is at right angles with the axis of rotation.* Then the plane of a planet's orbit must be at right angles with the axis of the cosmical sphere. And that is to say that the plane of the planet's orbit and the plane of the cosmical equator must be exactly coincident. There can be *no* inclination of the one plane to the other.

In the nebular theory the only force operating to give the detached planet an orbital motion is the centrifugal force. Could we find other planetary bodies occupying situations in space outside this plane, we should then have in gravitation a force by which the planetary orbit might be deflected from the plane of original rotation; but we are obliged to exclude all such suppositions. We must keep in mind that "*All the marvelous uniformities of the solar system are but the progeny of that primitive impulse which originated the grand rotation.*"

That there *are* perturbations in the orbital movements of the planets which can be traced to their mutual attractions, and that some of these perturbations are lateral, is known to all astronomers. And so carefully has this subject been studied that, by the perturbations of Uranus, Leverrier and Adams, independently, calculated the location of the planet Neptune, which, as yet, was unseen.

But has any one estimated the disturbing force of the attraction of one of the fixed stars upon one of the planets? Will any one aver, as a fact, that such stellar attraction does so affect the movements of a planet as to change the plane of its orbit? The advocates of the Nebular Hypothesis do not, so far as we know, make any such claims. All planetary perturbations, then, must arise from *planetary attractions*. But if the nebular theory be true, there never can arise such a collocation of the planetary masses as would give rise to orbital inclinations.

The grand rotation of the original mass elevates the *cosmical equator*. It does not—it cannot elevate any other region so much as that. If a ring could be produced at all it must be exactly over the equator, and its mass must extend equally on both sides of it. Thus equipoised, the attraction of the original mass will not disturb its equilibrium. There is no *other* body whose attraction will sensibly affect it.

Its own momentum, after it is detached, will carry it in the direction given by the projectile force. The centrifugal force projects it in a plane which is at right angles to the axis of rotation. Then it must forever move in that plane, unless some *other* force lays hold of it to turn it aside. But where is that plane? No matter where. If ever there was an original cosmical sphere revolving axially, and giving birth to planetary masses by the operation of the centrifugal force, then those planetary masses must have been projected in the equatorial plane of that cosmical sphere, and there we are authorized to look for them to-day.

All causation is within. Planetary history is a history of evolutions.

Looking at the solar system from this standpoint of *theory*, (the nebular theory,) and recalling to mind the unchanging *law* of centrifugal projection, we are prepared to find uniformities. Nay, we demand uniformities. Nothing but uniformities will meet the requirements of the theory and of the law. We are advertised that there are *marvelous* uniformities. "Each has continued to revolve in an orbit which marks the periphery of the parent mass at the time of the planet's separation. All continue to revolve in the same direction as the parent mass and the resultant sun." Wonderful coincidences! Yet we expected them. Knowing that a world was projected from the parent mass *by the centrifugal force*, we could not for a moment dream that it could move in any *other* direction than that of the parent sphere. If the axial rotation of the cosmical sphere was from west to east, then the orbital rotation of the planetary mass *must be* from west to east. It will be marvelous, indeed, if it be in any other direction. And, if it take an axial rotation also, (as it probably will,) then that axial rotation will also be from west to east. The first-born planet will be found moving in the plane of the cosmical equator, and its own equatorial plane will be coincident with its orbital plane. And the next planet will revolve in the same plane; and the next, and the next. All planetary motion will be in one plane. It must be so upon the fundamental postulates of the Nebular Hypothesis. The theory must abide by its own postulates.

To assume that the direction of the axial rotation of the original cosmical sphere has undergone a change, is to assume a material point contrary to the law. To assume that the orbital or axial rotation of a planet has departed from its original plane, is also to assume a material point contrary to the law.

If the Nebular Hypothesis be dismissed, and we conceive of a planetary system in which, from the first, there is axial motion in different planes, and orbital motion in different planes, then we can see how there may arise changes of motion out of which shall come such phenomena as the precession of the equinoxes for instance. But on the principles of the Nebular Hypothesis we cannot admit the possibility of any such phenomena.

Let us now institute a more detailed examination of the solar system, with special reference to the *direction* of planetary motion. We commence our examination at the center of the system, because, by the terms of the theory "the sun is only the residual portion of the cosmical mass, still maintaining an inconceivably high temperature, simply because so vast a body of matter has not yet had time to cool off."—*Winchell.*

We are fortunate in finding the "residual portion of the cosmical mass;" and it is only fair to acknowledge that we find—

1st. That it is very hot.

2d. That it is very light—only a little heavier than water.

3d. That it is still a vast body, for its volume is five hundred times as great as the combined volumes of all the planets, and its mass is seven hundred and forty-five times as great as theirs. It is as if a mass of seven hundred and forty-six pounds had lost one pound.

4th. That, huge as it is, it is in motion on its axis.

And this last circumstance is what we are just now most concerned to observe. At present we care nothing about the *rate*, but we notice particularly the *direction* of its motion.

The sun rotates from west to east. Not exactly from west to east, as we see west and east on the earth, but in a general sense.

Now this axial rotation of the "residual portion," we assume, must be the original cosmical rotation, at least as to *direction*.

If it be not the original direction of the grand rotation what has changed it?

All motion generates force. Force can only be overcome by force.

Given the cosmical mass in motion in any direction, we cannot conceive of a change in the direction of that motion without the expenditure of adequate force. What force *could* change the direction of the axial rotation of the sun? We have also shown that, on the principles of the nebular theory, there could be no change of plane of a planet's orbit.

The direction of the rotation of the cosmical mass is therefore known. We have only to follow the plane of the sun's equator out into the heavens to the distance of Neptune and we will see exactly where the "periphery of the parent mass" was "at the time of the planet's separation."

Now watch the progress of Neptune. Does it keep along that plane? No, it is north of it. But it is approaching it. Now it is in it. But it crosses it, and goes on south of it. But it comes back again and recrosses it. And so, period after period, it crosses and recrosses the plane of the cosmical equator.

How was Neptune produced? By the centrifugal force? How, then, is the plane of his orbit inclined to the plane of the cosmical equator nine degrees?

We think this must be an illusion, and we proceed. We shall find Uranus, Saturn, Jupiter, and Mars, all revolving in the same plane, the plane of the cosmical equator.

Preposterous! Reader, did you say that? Why preposterous? Because every body knows that the planetary orbits are *all* inclined to the plane of the sun's equator. Indeed. Then, in the light of the *facts* our expectation *is* preposterous. *But by the premises of the nebular theory our expectation is only reasonable.*

What shall we do? If we take the facts we must throw away the theory, unless the facts can in some way be accounted for.

There are two things we cannot do: we cannot set aside the facts, and we cannot destroy the law of centrifugal projection. No. We must admit the facts: we must adhere to the law. It is a law of universal application.

The centrifugal force acts at right angles to the axis of rotation. It never acts otherwise. This law of motion cannot be subordinated to a theory of world formation. If the theory cannot abide the test of the law, so much the worse for the theory.

Sometimes the advocates of the nebular theory speak of the planetary masses as being "torn away" from the cosmical mass, and yet none of them really contemplate the act of detaching as any thing but an effect of the centrifugal force. No outside force is alleged. The centrifugal force, which accumulated in the peripheral matter, alone has the credit of detaching it. Therefore the detaching force is the *directive* force, which the planet must obey.

What, then, is the direction in which each of the planets moves? And how do they agree with the original grand rotation?

The planetary orbits are all inclined to the plane of the sun's equator, as follows:—

Mercury, 14 degrees; Venus, 13 degrees; Earth, 7½ degrees; Mars, 9 degrees; Jupiter, 8½ degrees; Saturn, 10 degrees; Uranus, 8 degrees; Neptune, 9 degrees.

The asteroids also belong to the solar system. How many there are of them we know not. It is conjectured that there may be several hundred, or even thousands, of them. They are small planets. They are revolving around the sun in orbits of varying eccentricity and inclination. One of them—Pallas—revolves in an orbit whose plane is inclined about forty degrees to the plane of the sun's equator.

One other class of objects demands our attention. The comets revolve around the sun, and though they are known to be exceedingly light, aeriform bodies, yet they must be recognized as erratic members of the cosmical system; wandering fragments of the attenuated world stuff; and our inquiry is incomplete if it do not ask, How did they originate? How were they cast off from the cosmical sphere?

We shall hardly make a separate theory for these bodies. They belong to that material fabric which we are studying. They contain the same elements, at least in part. They have orbital motions. They began their career under some impulse. What was it? If the solar system came out of an original cosmical condition, like that portrayed by the nebular theory, then the comets were once portions of the nebular mass, and in some way were projected from it. And we must refer their separate existence to the centrifugal force.

Well, in what direction do they move? In many directions. Some have a direct motion from west to east in planes only slightly inclined to the ecliptic. Some revolve at nearly right angles to the plane of the ecliptic, and others have a retrograde rotary motion.

And now, having taken this general view of the orbital motions of the solar system, what is our conclusion? Have we found the marvelous uniformities? Have we not rather found marvelous variations?

The advocates of the nebular theory are not ignorant of these variations—nay, we should say when referring them to that theory, these discordances. How, then, do they explain them or account for them? They do not account for them. They appear to regard them as unimportant trifles. They seem amazed at the general uniformity of the system, as if uniformities were not to be expected from the premises of the theory. They seem to be totally unimpressed by the exceptional motions.

Thus far we have considered only the motions of the primary planets. Let us now look at the orbital rotation of the satellites. The satellites, according to the theory, were projected from the planetary masses in the same manner in which the planets were projected from the original mass.

If they were so projected, we are authorized, by the law, to look for them in the planes of their planets' equators.

Taylor, in the discussion of "The nature and origin of force," refers to the moon as "an outlying portion of the earth's former equator." But the moon's orbit cuts the plane of the earth's equator at an angle of nearly twenty-nine degrees. The satellites of Uranus and Neptune exhibit a startling exception to the general order of rotation. In these cases the direction of the rotation is reversed, the satellites *moving from east to west.*

Professor Winchell sees no difficulty here, however, and nothing incompatible with the nebular theory. He says, "In fact, the plane of the satellites is tilted up at an angle which exceeds the perpendicular by about eleven degrees; thus the whole system is nearly *inverted*, and the motion of the satellites, like that of the hands of a watch lying face downward, seem to be reversed. A moment's reflection will convince us, however, that this is an illusion. The motion is normal. The attitude of the system only is extraordinary."

It only requires "a moment's reflection." "In fact, the plane of the satellite is tilted up." "The attitude *only* is extraordinary." Now, to us, this seems the veriest trifling. Why is not this *tilting up* accounted for? That it *is* tilted up is a circumstance that is incompatible with the Nebular Hypothesis. What caused it? How came the *attitude* to be extraordinary? The *attitude only* is certainly a matter of some moment. The Uranian system is not contemptible for its magnitude. It would require something of a force to invert that system.

One would suppose that an event of so much importance in *planetary history* should have a little more serious consideration than a "moment's reflection."

It is a fact that if the planets originated as

this theory claims, the plane of these satellites *has* been tilted up. Then some force must have tilted it.

It is not necessarily the province of the astronomer to account for these exceptional motions. He has met all his legitimate obligations when he has fully described them. But when an astronomer assumes the *rôle* of *historian of planetary evolution*, then it becomes incumbent on him to account for every exception to that order which his historical theory requires.

But Winchell alleges that the " motion is normal," yet what he means by *normal* in this connection we are at a loss to understand. Does he mean simply that the motion is rotary? That the satellites revolve in orbits? Or does he mean that they revolve in the same direction in which the parent planets perform their axial rotation? If so, does he not *assume* the direction of their rotation? To our mind that motion is normal which is according to known laws—laws of velocity and laws of direction.

If a body is put in motion by the explosive force of gunpowder, and it is made to take the direction of a certain object, we consider its motion normal so long as its flight is such as could have been *calculated* for it by one knowing its weight and its initial velocity; but if it go to the right or left, and no cause can be assigned for this change in its direction, can we say it is normal? But if the flight of the projectile be at a right angle with the line of projection, or if it should fly toward the rear, what *would* we say? Who could explain that?

In ancient times the sling was employed in warfare. But the skill of the slinger consisted chiefly in two elements: the ability to revolve the sling in the perpendicular plane, and the tact to release the projectile at the exact point in the circle, at which its direction would be toward its object.

The centrifugal force must do the rest. Now suppose the plane of rotation to be perpendicular, and yet the flight of the projectile to be greatly deflected to the right or left. Is that a normal motion?

In the case of Uranus and its satellites the latter are affectionately contemplated by the nebular theory as the children of the former.

The process of their derivation is particularly described. "Similarly the planetary masses detached rings which became their satellites." "But what again of our family of infant planets? Each sprang forth, a globe of igneous vapor, like their common mother. Each began to repeat the process of cooling, condensation, and accelerated rotation. In the cases of the larger, the cooling had not reached the point of liquefaction before the rotation had become sufficiently rapid to detach from one to seven rings, which in turn became satellites revolving about their planets. The larger planets have had time to detach the greater number of rings. Our earth threw off but one, and became too rigid to repeat the process.

"Mars, Uranus, and Mercury—all smaller than the earth—attained the rigid condition before their acquired velocity had separated the periphery. Their nights are consequently unillumined by the presence of a moon."— WINCHELL, *Sketches of Creation.*

Notice in every case, the manner of producing a planet is the same. The centrifugal force detaches a ring from the periphery of the revolving cosmical mass. The one thing which is essential to the accomplishment of this work is "sufficient velocity." When detachment takes place, all that sufficient velocity attends the detached mass. It goes forward in the route determined for it by the centrifugal force. But the satellites of Uranus decline to obey the law, and turn back on their course, and making a circuit, so to speak, make an oblique and retrograde path of their own, without law and without warrant.

It is *not* an illusion. It is a fact.

The satellites are not revolving where they must revolve if the nebular theory be true. And the fact is against the theory.

The same fact is observable in the satellite of Neptune. Its one satellite revolves around the planet from east to west. The first born of satellites, like the first born of man, reverses nature's own decree, sets at naught the law, and sports itself in opposition to authority.

The phenomenon also remains unaccounted for by the nebular theory. Rather, we should say, the fact stands against the theory and cannot be reconciled with it. Disappointment meets us at every step.

We started out to examine the actual motions of the solar system, assured that all planetary motion was the progeny of an original grand rotation of the cosmical mass; and hence concluding that it would be found obedient to the *laws of centrifugal projection.* We find the planetary motions random motions. We cannot reconcile them with the law. There is not a single instance of conformity to it. Such a thing as uniformity is not to be found. Planets revolve in planes that are slightly inclined to each other; comets dash through the planetary regions in orbits whose planes are perpendicular to those of the planets; asteroids swing about in many directions, cutting through other planetary planes at large angles; and satellites crown the bewildering confusion with absolutely retrograde movements. We can come to but one conclusion. The origin of planetary motions is not accounted for by the nebular theory. There is not a single instance of orbital motion that is what it must be to be in harmony with the fundamental postulates of that theory.

We have yet to consider the axial rotation of the planets and their satellites.

The axial rotation of a planet, according to the theory, as we have before seen, is the product of the same impulse which gives it an orbital motion. And this, it has been claimed, is at once illustrated and proven by Plateau's celebrated experiment.

Admitting the truth of this theory, we submit that it would result that the orbital plane of each planet and satellite must coincide with its equatorial plane. Then the proposition which we submitted early in this chapter would be verified; *all planetary motion must be found in one plane.* True, then, there would be no changes of seasons on the planet's surface; but what of that? The grand rotation is not an intelligent designer, prompted by benevolent considerations to shape a system for the benefit of any existences whatever. The grand rotation is simply an inexorable projector of worlds. It can only project them in one plane. It can go no further.

But the planets do not revolve in one plane. Every planetary orbit cuts the plane of the sun's equator at some angle. The satellites do not revolve in that one plane. Their orbits not only cut the plane of the sun's equator, but they also cut the planetary orbits. So, also, the axial motion disregards the law. The equatorial plane of every planet, so far as we know, cuts across the orbital plane. The inclinations, at which they cross, vary greatly, but the least of them is too great to harmonize with the nebular theory.

The following table exhibits the inclination of orbital plane to equatorial plane: Mercury, 70 degrees; Venus, 75 degrees; Earth, $23\frac{1}{2}$ degrees; Mars, $28\frac{1}{2}$ degrees; Jupiter, 3 degrees; Saturn, $26\frac{3}{4}$ degrees. The inclination in the cases of Uranus and of Neptune is unknown.

Looking at these figures we are constrained again to ask, Are these the marvelous uniformities that were announced as observable in the solar system? Are they not unaccountable diversities? What force tilted up the axis of each planet, so that its axial rotation shall be in another plane than that of its orbit? How is it that Venus has been tilted up to the extent of seventy-five degrees? True, Venus is not a very large planet, and yet it certainly would require *force* to put it in motion, and an equal force to stop it when once in motion. But it must have been moved seventy-five degrees, and then stopped, for its axis is fixed in direction, that is, it is parallel to itself, at all points of the orbit. The same remarks will apply to all the planets whose axial inclination is known.

Another problem requires solution by the principles of the nebular theory:—*What must be the ratio of the axial to the orbital rotation of any given planet?*

We think it evident, that if the centrifugal force projected a planet into space, the orbital velocity of the detached mass, at the moment of detachment, must have been the equatorial velocity of the mass from which it was detached. Exactly that: no more, no less.

Now if we suppose the detached mass to be gathered together into a planetary sphere while moving forward in the tangent of the circle of rotation, we must allow that it will acquire an axial rotation, because its outer portion, that is, that portion which is farthest from the axis of the original rotation, must move faster than that portion which is nearest that axis, and so the planet must turn upon its own center. And the difference between its exterior velocity and its interior velocity would determine the rate of its axial rotation. The more the direction of the planet's flight is deflected from the tangent toward the circle the less would be that difference; and, therefore, it would follow that the more circular the orbit of a planet the less rapid ought to be its axial revolution, if it has arisen on this plan, which is the plan of the nebular theory. But in any event it will be seen that a definite ratio must have existed between a planet's orbital motion and its axial motion. A very simple geometrical figure would illustrate this proposition. Moreover, the nebular theory *proceeds* on the assumption that the same force, that is, the centrifugal force, has given to the planets severally both axial and orbital motion; and it is for this reason—because a law of development is supposed to exist—that a history of planetary origin is supposed to be possible. And thus, Winchell says, "This community of conditions, this unanimous obedience to *one code of physical laws*, implies that all these bodies are urged onward through *a common history*, and have probably had their starting point in one common state of matter." "Thus the present state of the solar system is a living picture of the entire history of a single planet."

We are searching for that code of physical laws. We know something of the laws of attraction, of the radiation of heat, of the velocity of falling bodies, of the centrifugal force; but here arises a case in which we think there must be a law regulating the relative rates of the two kinds of planetary motion. We do unhesitatingly affirm that if the planets have been projected from a revolving mass, as the nebular theory assumes that they have been, then there must be a mathematical ratio between their orbital rotation and their axial rotation, and any ordinary geometrician—assuming the diameter of the cosmical sphere to be a definite measure, and the diameter of the detached mass to be another definite measure, and knowing the detaching velocity—can calculate what the axial rotation must be. If the orbital rotation be slow, the axial rotation must be correspondingly slow. If the orbital rotation be rapid, the axial rotation must be correspondingly rapid. We have a right, then, in advance, to predict one thing respecting the axial rotations of the planets, to wit, that they will be found to increase in velocity as we approach the sun, as we know that their orbital velocity increases.

Do we find our prediction verified as we travel inward from Neptune? The following table exhibits the actual rates of these two kinds of rotary motion in all the planets whose axial motion is known:—

TABLE.

Rate of Orbital Motion.	Rate of Axial Motion.
Saturn...... .0014 degrees.	34.5 degrees per hour.
Jupiter...... .0034 "	36. " " "
Mars .... .021 "	15.7 " " "
Earth....... .041 "	15. " " "
Venus....... .066 "	15.3 " " "
Mercury .... .17 "	14. " " "

Thus it appears that there is no common ratio existing between these two kinds of motion. The large, remote planets, Jupiter and Saturn, with comparatively slow orbital motion have very high rates of axial rotation, and Mercury, with the highest rate of orbital, has the lowest rate of axial, rotation. These facts are inexplicable. At least they are inexplicable on the principles of the nebular theory. If that theory were true, these things could not be. The facts are against the theory.

CHAPTER VII.

DENSITIES.

Probable disposition of the cosmical matter on theoretical principles.

AMONG the facts of the solar system which are supposed to corroborate the nebular theory, the advocates of the theory find this—the density of the outer planets is less than that of those nearer the sun. Professor Winchell says: "It is reasonable to suppose that the older planets are composed of a smaller proportion of the denser elements than the newer planets, since they are formed from the peripheral portions of the original fire-mist, while it is likely the denser portions gathered about the center, and entered, to a larger extent, into the constitution of later rings. The lower specific gravity of the older planets may be partly attributed to this cause."

We think it evident, that in a spherical body, whose particles are free to move among each other—situated as the nebular theory supposes the cosmical sphere to have been situated—the matter of least specific gravity must be most remote from the center, and the matter of greatest specific gravity must be gathered about the center. This is exactly what we see fluid matter of all kinds do, under ordinary circumstances, on the earth. Matter in a fluid state, when thrown together, arranges itself into different strata, unless chemical combination take place and prevent such arrangement. For the most dense will sink to the lowest place, and lift out whatever lighter matter occupied the place; the matter of next greatest density will rest on the denser, and so on upward; the less dense will be supported by the more dense, until, at the top, will be found the least dense of all.

At ordinary temperatures mercury, water, and various oils afford familiar illustrations of this law. Thus mercury will settle through water, and will support it. Water will settle through air, and will support it. And thus we may conceive of the sublimated materials which composed the original cosmical mass, obeying their resident gravitative force, and gradually forming distinct strata; and especially so, since the elements existed hypothetically in a dissociated state. Moreover, since, as Winchell truly intimates, "the states of matter are but the product of temperature and pressure," and since pressure is known in certain cases to counteract temperature, we may conceive of the denser elements, which go to the center, as subjected to pressure, which would change them from the vaporous to the liquid condition, while the remote lighter elements still remained in the gaseous condition. If, then, the cosmical sphere be supposed to have a rotary motion, we shall readily see that the lighter elements must be more powerfully affected by that motion, because they are nearest the surface of the revolving sphere. We are willing to adopt stronger language than Winchell employs, and say, *It must be so.*

As the water would rise through mercury, as air would rise through water, and as the lighter hydrogen gas would rise through air, so it would seem the lighter cosmical elements must have risen to the higher, that is, the outer regions; and as it was of the *peripheral* matter that each world was successively formed, the older planets must have been, at the time of their formation, the lighter planets, if formed in the manner set forth in the nebular theory. Then the oldest planet must have been formed of the lightest matter, and its satellite must have been formed of the lightest of that lightest matter. The next oldest planet must have been composed of the lightest of the residual matter, and its satellites must have been composed of the lightest of that lightest residual matter, and so on.

Yes, we can only agree with Winchell in this position, unless we go farther than he, and add, *there must be a regular gradation of densities in the planetary system.* Theoretically, no variation of densities is admissible, except a regular gradation from the *least* dense in the most remote to the *most* dense in the planet nearest the sun ; but *such* a gradation seems to be theoretically necessary on the premises assumed by the nebular theory. But let us suppose that the elements composing the cosmical mass were so affected by the inconceivably high temperature that the dissociation was attended with promiscuous intermixture, even to the outmost limits of the mass so that the whole mass was of uniform density, what effect must follow, theoretically, in the condition of each of the planetary masses? In that case, as in the other, we must still affirm that at the time of separation the planets must have been of regularly graded densities. Moreover, we are happily able in this case to tell, with very considerable accuracy, *what* the ratio of the density of each planetary mass must have been to that of the next preceding, and to any, indeed, of the whole number. For the nebular theory assumes that the orbits of the planets mark the limits of the cosmical sphere at the times when the respective planetary masses were detached. Grant this assumption. Then it follows that whatever the density of the cosmical matter was at the time of the separation of the Neptunian mass, by the contraction of the sphere to the limit marked by the orbit of Uranus, the *volume* of the cosmical sphere was shrunken to less than one fourth its previous measure. That sphere, of which the orbit of Neptune is the equatorial line, is 4.8 times as large as that whose equator is measured by the orbit of Uranus. But the contraction of volume is the condensation of the matter. If, then, the elements be supposed to have remained dissociated and intermixed, so that the whole mass was of uniform density at the time that the Uranian mass was detached, it is evident, that after allowing for the absence of the Neptunian mass, the matter of the Uranian system was more than four and a half times as dense as that of Neptune. But after detaching the Uranian mass the cosmical sphere again contracted to limits marked by the orbit of Saturn, and then the Saturnian mass was detached, and its matter was eight and a half times as dense as that of Uranus, and thirty-eight times as dense as that of Neptune.

We shall hereafter have occasion to refer to this point again, in speaking of the relative masses of the planets. It is not necessary, therefore, to extend our examination further into details at this stage of our inquiry. We have, we think, made it clear to every intelligent reader, that upon the assumption of uniform density of the cosmical substance, and the formation of worlds on the plan of the nebular theory, the second planetary mass must have been four and a half times as dense as the first, the third eight and a half times as dense as the second; and these three planetary masses were, in their density, as 1. 4½. 38. These numbers, it should be remembered, indicate the *original planetary densities.* Now the *present* actual densities are not supposed to be like the original densities, because the same processes that increased the density of the original cosmical sphere are supposed to have increased the density of each planetary mass also. Moreover, on the supposition that the contraction of the mass was the result of the cooling of the mass, it is evident that the small planetary masses must have contracted with a rapidity as many times greater than that of the parent mass as they were times smaller than that.

Now the Neptunian mass was only $\frac{1}{20,000}$ part of the original cosmical mass. It would, therefore, cool off twenty thousand times as fast as the original mass, and while the original mass was cooling and contracting to the limit at which its density was four and a half times as great as at first, the planetary mass would cool off and contract 4½×20,000, or ninety thousand times as much. So we are authorized to say that at the time of the separation of the Uranian mass the mass of Neptune was twenty thousand times as dense as Uranus, and ninety thousand times as dense as at its own birth.

In like manner, after the separation of the Uranian mass, three masses were undergoing the same process of cooling and contracting until the Saturnian mass was detached. The Uranian mass is about $\frac{1}{25,000}$ of the residual cosmical mass. Therefore it will cool and contract twenty-five thousand times as fast as the parent body. But the parent body contracts so much that its density is eight and a half times as great as it was when Uranus was detached. The density of Uranus must, therefore, be 8×25,000, or two hundred thousand times as great as it was at the time of its detachment, and twenty-five thousand times as great as the density of the Saturnian mass. And so, through unknown ages, the planetary masses have been cooling off and their density increasing.

Now this process of cooling and contracting would produce these proportionate effects for a limited period. But the time would come in the history of each separate mass that it would cease to shrink perceptibly, and thenceforward the relative densities would not be referable to temperature as their cause.

With these preliminary reflections we are prepared to make an examination of the actual densities of the planetary masses.

It is a fact that the remote planets are less dense than those nearer the sun. The density of Neptune is $\frac{9}{16}$; that of Uranus is 1.

According to the nebular theory Neptune is the oldest of the planets. The period that intervened between the time of its formation and that of the formation of Uranus no one pretends to know, but it is assumed that it was an immense period. We may be sure it was millions of ages, for in that period the cosmical sphere contracted from a diameter of six thousand millions of miles to one of three thousand five hundred millions of miles. Then Uranus was thrown off, and since that time they have been cooling and contracting together. Now have these two planets reached that point of congelation at which the density is not indicative of temperature, or have they not?

According to the nebular theory the three factors—*original density, original volume,* and *time*—are to be considered as determining the present density of a planet. Of these three factors we know exactly nothing. It is the practice of nebular theorists, however, when difficulties arise, to assume that they would speedily disappear could we only know the truth about original *volumes* and *time*.

The present densities of Neptune and Uranus, as we have seen, are $\frac{9}{10}$ and 1. We have also seen that there was a time, if this theory be admitted, when the density of Neptune was twenty thousand times as great as that of Uranus, and since that time the two bodies have been cooling off and contracting together. How is it, then, that Uranus has overtaken and passed by Neptune, so that now the density of Uranus is the greater? Shall we account for it by alleging the inferior mass of Uranus? As their masses are to each other as thirty-three to twenty-five, we submit, for the present, that the explanation has been found.

In going from Neptune to Uranus we went from a less density to a greater, and we have had an explanation of the fact. We now pass on and examine the density of Saturn. We remember that the cosmical matter out of which the Saturnian mass came was eight and a half times as dense as that out of which Uranus came. How is it, then, that we find Saturn's density only three fourths as great as that of Uranus? The answer is ready: Saturn is a younger and a larger body than Uranus, so that, though her original density was eight and a half times as great as that of Uranus, yet at the time of Saturn's birth Uranus had already attained considerable age, so great, indeed, that during the existence of Uranus the cosmical mass had acquired a density eight and a half times that with which Uranus started out. But during all that time Uranus was outstripping the parent mass in the race of condensation, because, being only $\frac{1}{25,000}$ as large as the parent mass, Uranus had condensed twenty-five thousand times as fast; and so, when Saturn sets out on his separate career, Uranus has already attained a density twenty-five thousand times as great as Saturn's. Of course, then, we must not expect Saturn to overtake Uranus in the process of condensation. Why not? For two reasons: 1. Because Uranus has so much the start. 2. Because Uranus, being so much smaller than Saturn, will *continue* to condense more rapidly than Saturn, and thus widen the distance between them. The mass of Saturn is more than seven times as great as that of Uranus. Uranus, therefore, will continue to cool off and condense seven times as fast as Saturn. Behold the result. Uranus, at the outset of Saturnian history, twenty-five thousand times as dense as Saturn, goes on through all the corresponding periods of planetary history seven times as rapidly as Saturn. We must change the form of our question and ask, How is it that Saturn is so heavy? How is it that the density of Saturn is so great? Unless we conclude that Uranus has long since reached an unchanging density, Saturn has a relative density many thousand times too great.

If we assume that Uranus and Neptune have both reached a condition of unchanging density, then their relative density ought to be as one to four, Neptune being one. But Neptune is nine tenths. Uranus is one.

Difficulties thicken, but let us go forward. Let us compare Saturn and Jupiter. The residual cosmical mass, after allowing the removal of all the matter of Saturn, was about three thousand five hundred times as great as the Saturnian mass. It had contracted to the limit marked by the orbit of Jupiter, and in so contracting its density was multiplied by six and a half. The matter of which Jupiter was constituted was, therefore, six and a half times as dense as the original matter of Saturn. But we must not forget that while the great parent mass was thus becoming six and a half times as dense, Saturn, which was only $\frac{1}{3,500}$ the mass of the cosmical parent, was increasing in density three thousand five hundred times as fast as the parent mass. At the very moment, therefore, that the Jovian mass was detached, the density of the Saturnian matter was three thousand five hundred times as great as the Jovian.

Now how will their contemporary history affect their relative densities? The mass of Jupiter is three hundred and one, while that of Saturn is ninety. Jupiter is, therefore, more than three times as large as Saturn. Then Saturn will contract and condense more than three times as fast as Jupiter. Will Jupiter ever overtake Saturn? Never until Saturn shall reach the point at which density undergoes little, if any, change. But Jupiter is already twice as dense as Saturn.

We found Saturn, when compared with Uranus, much too *dense* for the theory. We now find Saturn too *light*. We ask Professor Winchell to account for these discrepancies. Compare which planet we will with Saturn on the premises of the nebular theory, we are mocked by the results.

In pursuing this line of inquiry we have followed exactly the line pursued by Winchell in comparing the earth and the moon. The following is *almost* a quotation: "Saturn is only one third as large as Jupiter, and, therefore, it will cool off three times as fast. Its historic periods will be correspondingly shorter. And it will pass through its various stages of refrigeration so much more rapidly."

There is no regular gradation of densities. There is no indication that there ever was such a gradation. The densities of the larger planets are inexplicable on the principles of the nebular theory. And it is immaterial which supposition we shall make—that the lighter cosmical matter was the peripheral matter, or that the cosmical matter was of uniform density—in either case we ought to find a regular gradation of densities in the planetary system, but we do not find it.

Saturn is especially inexplicable. Associated with his elder brother, Uranus, in comparison he puts on an extravagant amount of gravity, a gravity utterly unbecoming his comparative youth. Associated with his younger brother, Jupiter, he is guilty of equally extravagant levity, utterly unbecoming to his advanced age. Young or old, Saturn fails to render support to the Nebular Hypothesis.

CHAPTER VIII.

DENSITIES—CONTINUED.

Existence of the same elements in different planets—In the sun—In the stars.

WE have assumed the existence of bodies of matter in gaseous condition in the heavens. We now further assume that these gaseous bodies are composed of elements that constitute the earth. We also suppose that these same elements are present in the sun and in the remotest fixed stars. These suppositions are not new; nor are they of special value to any cosmical theory. And yet the advocates of the nebular theory have recently experienced wonderful ecstasies from the fact that the spectroscope had assured us, to some extent, of the truth of this old supposition, and the existence, in the different planets, of the same elements has been mentioned as a ground of belief in the nebular theory. But does the admitted fact give support to the theory? Who has ever raised a question that the sun and planets were material bodies? Who has denied that the stars were material bodies? Who has denied the materiality of the *nebulæ?*

But does the fact of materiality prove "a common origin" of all these bodies in the sense in which those words are used in the nebular theory? Admitting that there are real *nebulæ* in the heavens—bodies of self-luminous vapor—does it follow that all planetary bodies were once masses of vapor? Supposing the original condition of each of the planetary bodies to have been igneous, does it follow that it must have been gaseous? But even if it did follow that the original condition was gaseous, would it follow that each body had been separated from the others by such a process of *mechanical evolution* as this nebular theory proposes? If the sun is composed of the same elements as the earth, does it follow that the earth has been derived from the sun? If all the planets be found to contain the same kind of matter that the sun contains, must we, therefore, conclude that all the planets were at the same period embraced in the sun? Then we must go further. *Identity of material elements existing in any two of the heavenly bodies proves a common origin, and at some time residence in one common mass.* We must, then, carry our generalization to the common origin of all the stellar bodies. True, some of them may be so far distant from us that we cannot *absolutely* determine their material constituents; yet, wherever we have been able to bring a star under the inquisition of the spectrum analysis it has given an answer touching its constituent elements; and we may be justified in assuming that the same elements that constitute the earth are present in every star as well as in the sun.

Then there must have been a time when the whole material universe, embracing the countless millions of stars, all the thousands of *nebulæ*, all the comets, and all the planets, were in the condition of igneous gas, filling all that inconceivably vast sphere within which the fixed stars are situated. Then there were no stars and no interstellar spaces. All was one vast furnace of inconceivably high temperature. The volume of the original cosmical mass, which is now formed into our solar system, must have been so much greater then than it was at the birth of Neptune, that a thousand cubic miles of it would not equal a grain in weight. Yes, accepting the nebular theory and its method of reasoning, we are conducted to this conclusion. The cosmical matter existed in an unbroken mass, as extensive as the universe. Look at the argument. The planets are composed of the same elements that compose the sun. Then they must have had a common origin. The sun contains the same elements which are contained by the stars. Then they must have had a common origin.

We might affirm that this sameness of constituent elements indicates a common origin in the fiat of one infinite Mind. We might *infer* the existence of a general *plan* in the adjustments of stellar relations. We might reach the conclusion that the general likeness of material features, so far as known, justifies the conclusion that an intelligent purpose was at the bottom, and an intelligent, constant supervision is exercised over the whole material universe by one Supreme Will. We might add that we know not what office the *nebulæ* have in the economy of nature, that if the universe be the work of Infinite Wisdom they have some office, and that if it be not, then *nothing* has any office, and all efforts to find a system of nature are idle.

But we will not urge such possible reflections. We repeat, as we have observed before, we are engaged in a strictly *material* study. We assume that there is a *material unity* in the universe. Whether any God exists or not, *there is material unity*, and we will not be diverted from our pursuit by any fear that our discoveries may possibly be inimical to religion. We have the proofs that worlds are bound together by gravitation in a great system. We have in light, which issues from a star so remote that it is years reaching us, the same actinic, the same illuminating, and the same thermal action that belongs to the light of our own sun, and we find it obedient to exactly the same laws of refraction and reflection.

Whatever else men may differ about, this would seem beyond dispute, all celestial and terrestrial bodies constitute one grand material unity. The material relations are intimate.

All material things are constantly acting upon each other.

But does it follow that all these bodies once slumbered in the bosom of a universal nebular mass? Does it follow that they have been mechanically evolved? Does it give probability to the suspicion of an original grand rotation of the whole universe as a gaseous mass, by which all existing *stars* and *nebulæ* became separated from each other? Does it follow that our solar system has thus separately been evolved? Not at all. Not one of all these facts of nature hints at any such thing.

But if we should concede the existence of the universe originally in such gaseous state, have we gained any thing for science? Nothing at all. It cannot possibly be lifted above the level of absolutely groundless speculation.

It is not history. When referred to it, the title "Planetary History" is a misnomer. Suppose we drift with this theory thus far, is it at all satisfactory? Whence the star dust? We want a history of the cosmical matter. Carry us to the beginning. Let us reach the source of the historic stream.

But, really, this nebular theory is not a planetary history. It is not a history of matter. It is destitute of all the elements of history. It is a congeries of stupendous assumptions, and it disregards at every step the simplest, plainest, and most thoroughly established facts and laws of material nature. Who can tell whether the primitive state of matter was gaseous or not? Is it not as easy to account for terrestrial changes on other suppositions as on that? But for the purpose of giving countenance to the theory of ring formations it would probably never have been mentioned. For the *nebular* theory the gaseous condition is necessary. There must be a gaseous condition of the cosmical matter, according to one form of the theory, so as to allow of condensation by the force of gravity, and the condensation by this force is supposed to have evolved the inconceivable heat.

Thus says HELMHOLTZ; "When the nebulous chaos first separated itself from other fixed-star masses, it must not only have contained all kinds of matter which was to constitute the future planetary system, but also, in accordance with our new law, (Helmholtz here refers to the "Principle of the conservation of force,") "the whole store of force which at one time must unfold therein its wealth of action. *Indeed, in this respect an immense dower was bestowed, in the shape of the general attraction of all the particles for each other.* This force, which on the earth exerts itself as gravity, acts in the heavenly space as gravitation. As terrestrial gravity, when it draws a weight downward, performs work and generates *vis viva*, so also the heavenly bodies do the same thing when they draw two portions of matter from distant regions of space toward each other. The chemical forces must also have been present, ready to act; but as these can only come into operation by the most intimate contact of the different masses, *condensation must have taken place before the play of chemical forces began.*

"Whether a still further supply of force, in the shape of heat, was present at the commencement, we do not know. At all events, by the law of the equivalence of heat and work wo find in the mechanical forces, existing at the time to which we refer, such a rich source of heat and light, that there is no necessity whatever to take refuge in the idea of a store of these forces originally existing.

"When, through condensation of the masses, their particles came into collision and clung to each other, the *vis viva* of their motion would be thereby annihilated, and must appear as heat.

"Already, in old theories, it has been calculated that cosmical masses must generate heat by their collision, but it was far from any body's thought to make even a guess at the amount of heat to be generated in this way. At present we can give definite numerical values with certainty."

After stating the problem and the method of solution, Helmholtz continues: "The result of this calculation is, that only about the four hundred and fifty-fourth part of the original mechanical force remains as such, and that the remainder, converted into heat, would be sufficient to raise a mass of water equal to the sun and planets taken together, not less than twenty-eight millions of degrees of the centigrade scale."

Tyndall only expresses the same meaning in another form of words when he says: "The potential energy of gravitation was the original form of all the energy in the universe."

We see, in the light of these quotations, how necessary to this form of the nebular theory the assumption of the original gaseity of matter is. If the cosmical matter was of *very great* tenuity—so great, indeed, that chemical forces could have no play—then there could be condensation; and, through condensation, *vis viva* or living force, or mechanical force; and, through the expenditure of the *vis viva*, heat; enough heat, indeed, to raise a body of water equal to the mass of all the bodies in the solar system to a temperature of twenty-eight million degrees centigrade. Two things the great philosopher of Bonn did not explain. He did not explain how matter could reach such tenuity without heat, and he did not explain what effect the developed heat would have on the density of the matter.

He also speaks of the "nebular chaos," as separating itself from the other fixed-star masses," but leaves us entirely in the dark as to the *mode* of the separation. Certainly, if it is the behoof of science to show how *planets* were separated from the "*nebular chaos*," it must be equally its behoof to show how the "nebular chaos" was separated from "the other fixed-star masses."

That form of the nebular theory advocated by WINCHELL, STERRY HUNT, and others, also assumes the existence of matter originally in the condition of a gas of great tenuity, but in this case the gaseity is the result of inconceivably high heat. To this we shall have occasion to refer hereafter, and only mention it now to show that the gaseous condition of the cosmical matter is alike necessary to both forms of the nebular theory; and also to remark that grave difficulties invest that form of the theory enunciated by Helmholtz which are avoided by Winchell, and it is therefore that we devote our attention chiefly to the theory as set forth by the latter as the more plausible theory.

CHAPTER IX.

PLANETARY HISTORY.

A magnificent picture—Progressive changes in structure—Discussion—Structure of the earth—The interior fires—Hopkins's theory—The lunar stage—Sir Charles Lyell—Experiments of Mr. Daniels with molten metals.

THE nebular theory, as a history of matter, follows the planetary masses into their separate and individual history. Cast off from the cosmical mass while yet inconceivably hot, they were self-luminous gaseous bodies. They could not at first be regarded as analogous to our sun. They would have to pass through a number of stages before they would reach the solar stage. But they contracted, and their axial rotation was accelerated and the satellite masses thrown off, as the planetary masses had been thrown off before. Thus the celestial fires were multiplied. Cosmical original, primary planetary masses, and secondary planetary masses were glowing with their own native heat together in the firmament.

But they came in time to be suns. Then they expired as suns, and the Saturnian stage came on. Just *where*, in the history, the temperature became such as to allow of chemical combinations, we are not informed. Perhaps this information is denied us for the purpose of leaving room for a healthful play of the imagination.

It is, however, assumed that chemical combination began at the surface, because it was here that the cooling was most rapid. Certainly we can imagine that it must have been very cold at the surface, or just outside of it. When chemical action began, and compounds were formed at the surface or in the higher regions, the compounds began immediately to fall toward the center of the mass. But they could not go far before they would meet a heat of dissociation, and their course would be arrested. More and more rapidly this process went on, and the cooling and contracting were accelerated. In process of time the cooling was carried to that extent that the elements, which were freely intermixed, sought chemical association, and combination generally took place throughout the mass.

Says Dr. Hunt: "So long as the gaseous condition of the earth lasted we may suppose the whole mass to have been homogeneous; but when the temperature became so reduced that the existence of chemical compounds at the center became possible, those which were most stable at the elevated temperature then prevailing would be first formed. Thus, for example, while the compounds of oxygen with mercury, or even with hydrogen, could not exist, oxides of silicon, aluminum, calcium, magnesium, and iron might be formed and condensed in a liquid form at the center of the globe. By progressive cooling, still other elements would be removed from the gaseous mass which would form the atmosphere of the non-gaseous nucleus."—*Chemistry of the Earth.*

Having an atmosphere thus theoretically provided for, an atmosphere of uncombined gases, and a central liquid nucleus, we are naturally led to the contemplation of the chemical combination of oxygen and hydrogen, and the beginning of a period of aqueous conflict with the interior heat. Winchell anticipates us here, as follows: "During a cosmic period the clouds accumulate, slowly shutting out the light of the sun, and copiously discharging their rains toward the planet. The rains, penetrating the lower strata of the atmosphere, are converted to vapor, and returned to the clouds, to be again condensed and precipitated. Every ascending particle of vapor carries off a portion of heat from the atmosphere, and promotes the cooling of the planet. But cosmic changes are slow, and ages must elapse while a tempest rages in mid air, which is quite unfelt upon the surface of the planet, save as the vivid lightnings shed a violet gleam over the arid surface, or the rolling thunders mark the time of the tempest's march. Gradually the line of conflict settles toward the heated crust. At length the rain strikes the crust. Then, after a period of increased excitement in the elements, a universal ocean begins to accumulate—a boiling, steaming, turbid ocean. After a further lapse of ages the cooling and accumulating waters lead to signs of exhaustion in the clouds. Light filters feebly through, and the lowest organisms appear in the sea. Then the clouds break, and the full sunlight and peaceful elements are the signal for advancing grades of organization."

This is history. That primitive impulse which originated the grand rotation has developed multiform energies, and that cosmical matter, whose tenuity was so great that several cubic miles would weigh less than a single grain, lies before us in massive rocks, underlying a universal ocean, surrounded by an atmosphere fitted to sustain some forms of organization.

Let us follow over this historical track, and try its credibility.

First of all we ask, *What authority have we in experimental science for the assumption that an inconceivably high temperature could be maintained in a cosmical mass of dissociated elements?*

What is temperature? Heat is simply *thermal activity* or a *form of motion*, which exhibits effects which are known as thermal. Temperature is the degree of that activity. Now we have no means of knowing what is the normal thermal state. But we know that there are certain laws of thermal evolution. We know that certain substances, when brought into contact *at certain temperatures*, will immediately rush into chemical combination. We know that the chemical combination, when it is effected, occasions the exhibition of heat. But at other temperatures we know that the same elements might remain imtermixed for long periods of time without combining, and that so long as they thus remained no heat will result from their intermixture. We know, also, that these same elements might be put into motion and brought suddenly into collision while moving in opposite directions, and that their mass motion would be converted into that molecular motion which we call heat.

But we do *not* know that the elements can all exist in a vaporous or gaseous condition without heat. And we do not know of any mode of producing such a heat as could effect so complete a sublimation of the elements as the nebular theory supposes to have existed. If these elements were put into the gaseous state by heat and intermixed, we may conceive of their remaining together in that state so long as the heat is maintained, but the heat must, in some way, be generated.

But in the hypothetical cosmical mass there is no generation of heat. No rational account of its origin is given. There is no chemical combination. It is too hot for that. Therefore chemical combination cannot account for the heat. It is not the contraction of the cosmical mass, for the contraction is the result of cooling. Whence the inconceivable heat of the *original* cosmical mass? What kind of activity could exist among elements chemically dissociated, and incapable of chemical combination, the manifestation of which would be a continued thermal state of inconceivably high temperature?

We have sought in the writings of the advocates of the nebular theory for some rational answer to these questions, and we have sought in vain. We have read with special interest "The Chemistry of the Earth." Surely, we said, we shall find a clew to the origin of the nebular temperature. So distinguished a physicist as Dr. Sterry Hunt will not pass this point unnoticed. But he does. He says: 'The nebulous matter is conceived to be so intensely heated as to be in the state of true gas or vapor." That is all the light we get on the subject, and that is just no light at all.

"The nebulous matter *is conceived* to be so intensely heated" by what? When we look at the rotation of planets in orbits we behold *movements*, for the *origin* of which this nebular theory professes to give us an historical account, pointing us to an axial rotation of a hypothetical cosmical mass as the original of the orbital planetary rotation.

When we turn our thoughts to this hypothetical cosmical mass, and consider its axial rotation, we behold a movement for which the nebular theory professes to render an account, assigning as its cause the cooling and contracting of the cosmical matter. But this "cooling of the matter" is simply the subsidence of molecular movements in the matter. Heat is molecular activity. Cold is molecular inactivity or rest. In this chain of causes we have now reached the most important of all. Here is the "primitive impulse which originated the grand rotation." It must be here, and we wish to know what it is.

Here is motion, molecular motion, more intense than any that is known in our day. It is more intense than that which exists in the sun. What is the cause of this motion? And how is this motion maintained? And why is this molecular motion supposed to subside first at the surface, where there is *nothing* to react upon it?

In our simplicity we have supposed that all motion implied the previous existence and the application of *force*. Molecular motion is not an exception to the rule, so far as we know. Then we are justified in demanding a cause, in some mentionable force, for the hypothetical high heat of the *original* cosmical matter. Here the nebular theory seems to us to leave the cosmical mass in a situation somewhat similar to that of Deacon Homespun's world. His world was as flat as a pancake. His world rested on rocks. These rocks rested on rocks. And those rocks rested on rocks; and, finally, "*Well, you simpleton, it's rocks all the way down.*" And thus the stability of the world is accounted for.

So, according to the nebular theory, we have a *world in motion*, and its motions are accounted for by referring them to an axial rotation of a cosmical mass. Then this axial rotation must be *accounted* for. And the theory assigns, as its cause, the cooling and contracting of the mass, which "Is conceived to be so intensely *heated* as to be in the state of a true gas or vapor." Here, in this indescribable heat, is the most stupendous motion of all, the molecular motion, which was capable of tearing in pieces the aggregate matter of the solar system, dissociating the elements, and giving to the mass so great tenuity that three cubic miles of the stuff should be less than one grain in weight, *and here the nebular theory leaves us uninformed as to the cause of this stupendous activity.* "Rocks all the way down." Just so, deacon; that is just as scientific as to say, "*Motion all the way back.*" We put *your* cosmical theory and this *nebular* theory in the same category as equally rational.

But we must follow the track of this cosmical history. If it does not inform us how the motion began, it does tell us something of what follows. Let us pass those periods during which the planetary masses were detached as gaseous bodies; let us hasten on, not stopping even to glance at the gaseous satellites, and let us not be delayed by the terrific elemental convulsions which took place when the elements awoke to the realization of their first love and rushed into each other's embrace, and let us look at the subdued, tempered, peopled earth, with its strong rocky crust, its broad oceans, and its vital atmosphere enveloping all. There have been mighty upheavals. Great mountain ranges have been built up, ocean beds have been depressed, the igneous rocks have been exposed to winter's frosts and parched by summer suns; pelted by torrents of acidulated rain, and worn by unrestrained hurricanes; and thus cracked, shivered, corroded, crushed, the waters have swept the disintegrated ruins down into the ocean. Again and again this process of evolution, disintegration, and transportation of rock material has been repeated.

The terrestrial stage has already lasted untold ages. Yet, even now, what the world was, is indicated to us by what it is. Within its crust is a globe of liquid fire. The crust itself is only a few miles in thickness. Here and there great openings afford to the curious a sight of the boiling hot elements.

These things prove what was the earth's former state. But all do not accept this interpretation of the facts of terrestrial history. Dr. Hunt says: "The effect of pressure upon materials like molten rocks would be such that solidification at a depth from the surface would take place at a temperature much higher than that required for their solidification at the surface. Hence, in opposition to the notion of a congealed layer, like ice, resting upon the surface of the molten globe, Hopkins, and with him Scrope, supposes solidification to have commenced at the center of the liquid mass, and to have advanced toward the circumference."

We shall not, therefore, be without excellent company if we venture to express a doubt that our earth has a superficial crust and an interior molten mass. We may be permitted the thought that we live on a globe which is chiefly solid, that the liquid portion is quite small in proportion to the whole mass, and that the portion that is molten with high heat is a still smaller portion than the lakes and seas that variegate the surface.

Dr. Hunt further remarks: "Apart from

these considerations, however, many of the best modern physicists and geologists have found numerous reasons for rejecting the popular notion which regards our globe as a liquid molten mass covered by a layer of twenty or thirty miles of solidified rock. The deductions of Hopkins from the phenomena of precession and nutation ; those of Pratt from the crushing force of immense mountain masses, like those of the Himalaya ; and those of Sir William Thompson from the tides, showing the great rigidity of the earth—all unite to prove that the earth, if not solid to the center, must have a firm and solid crust several hundred miles in thickness. Under these conditions, if there still exist a liquid center, it must, so far as superficial phenomena are concerned, be as inert as if it were not. We are thus prepared to accept the conclusions to which the line of argument leads us, and admit that our globe solidified from the center."
—*Chemistry of the Earth.*

If the earth solidified from the center, then it is solid at the center. How far outwardly from the center does the solidification extend? Evidently it must extend outwardly to the surface, or we must suppose a solid globe within a molten envelope, which itself is inclosed within a solid shell. It would be a curious problem to determine what would be the result of such an arrangement as this.

But it would seem that if the center, and from the center outward for any great distance, is solid, there is nothing to justify the conclusion that an intermediate, continuous, concentric chamber, so to speak, is filled with matter in original molten condition.

The nebular theory, as set forth by Winchell, finds all its contractions arising from the cooling of the mass. The internal fires are inclosed within the rocky crust. Very gradually the heat is being radiated, because it is only slowly conducted to the surface. But the crust is thickening constantly by the cooling of that portion of the interior mass which is in contact with the crust.

The present condition of the moon is supposed to be such as that toward which the earth is progressing. There the theory beholds a world whose interior fires have quite burned out; whose oceans, and seas, and atmosphere have been sucked up by the rocks;

a world which is now "a *fossil* world, an ancient cinder, suspended in the heavens; once the seat of all the varied and intense activities which now characterize the surface of our earth, but in the present period a realm of silence and stagnation."

And the same process of refrigeration which has brought the moon to a state of desolation and solitude is now going on within and upon the earth. Thus the history runs, from the inconceivable heat and the attenuated gaseous condition, to the denser vapor; then to the liquid; then to the solid, (but still the white hot solid;) afterward to the red hot; afterward to the blackened, igneous rock, and on to the cooled exterior, and the molten, fervid interior, and the end, is to be a cold, cheerless desolation.

How much of this theory owes its existence to the fact that we know of the existence of subterranean fires, and lakes of liquid lava? From molten lava to the assumption of an original molten earth is not a very extravagant flight of the imagination; and from the molten earth to the igneous nebular condition is not a very difficult flight, especially if one may rest the wings of his fancy on real *nebulæ* in the heavens.

But a molten earth is an *assumed* point. Though deemed one of the most important of the data, it is only an assumption. Take this away, and what becomes of the theory? We are quite sure that this molten earth is really a *necessity* to the theory. *What else but the internal fires prevents the rocks from absorbing the terrestrial oceans and the terrestrial atmosphere?*

And yet this molten earth is taken away and rendered absolutely unavailable by the computations and reasonings of "many of the best physicists and geologists," and they do reject this "popular notion" of a "liquid, molten mass surrounded by a layer of twenty or thirty miles of solidified rock."

These physicists are—at least some of them are—men who accept the Nebular Hypothesis. Yet they find that the present earth is *not* a molten globe, enveloped by a thin crust, but that it must be considered as almost entirely solid. And this they do mathematically, and not with loose generalizations.

The question with them is not, "What *was*

the earth once?" but "What is it now?" To this question they make answer, and the answer is, "The earth is so nearly solid, that if there be any portion near the center that is molten, it is, so far as external phenomena are concerned, as inert as if it were not." And then Dr. Hunt comes in with his chemical data, and shows that this condition of central solidity is not inconsistent with the law of solidification of metals and metallic compounds under pressure.

We are warranted, therefore, not only in the conclusion that the fluidity of the central earth is *not* proven, but that, even if the whole mass were once fluid from the effect of heat, it is not fluid now. And if not fluid now, then all the theoretic history, based on the assumption of its present fluidity, fails with the assumption.

Sir CHARLES LYELL presents another view of the subject. He says: "The conditions of the problem are wholly altered when we reason about a fluid nucleus, as we must do if it be assumed that the heat augments from the surface to the interior according to the rate observed in mines. For when the heat of the lower portion of a fluid is increased, a circulation begins throughout the mass by the ascent of hotter and the descent of colder currents. And this circulation, which is quite distinct from the mode in which heat is propagated through solid bodies, must evidently occur in the supposed central ocean, if the law of fluids and of heat are the same there as upon the surface. In Mr. Daniel's experiments for obtaining a measure of the heat of bodies at their point of fusion, he invariably found that it was impossible to raise the heat of a large crucible of melted iron, gold, or silver a single degree beyond the melting point so long as a bar of the respective metals was kept immersed in the fluid portions. So, in regard to other substances, however great the quantities fused, their temperatures could not be raised while any solid pieces immersed in them remained unmelted, every accession of heat being instantly absorbed during their liquefaction. These results are, in fact, no more than the extension of a principle previously established, that so long as a fragment of ice remains in water we cannot raise the temperature of the water above thirty-two degrees Fahrenheit. There must be a continual tendency toward a uniform heat, and until this were accomplished by the interchange of portions of fluid of different densities the surface could not begin to consolidate. Nor on the hypothesis of primitive fluidity can we conceive any crust to have been formed until the *whole planet* had cooled down to about the temperature of incipient fusion."—*Principles of Geology.*

Lyell also refers to the opinions of M. POISSON, as set forth in a memoir to the Academy of Sciences in 1837, on the solid parts of the globe, and adds: " In this memoir he controverts the doctrine of the high temperature of a central fluid on similar grounds to those above stated. He imagines that if the earth ever passed from a liquid to a solid state by the radiation of heat, the central nucleus must have begun to cool and consolidate first."

One consideration more occurs to our mind as worthy of record on this subject. Assuming the fluidity of the earth, and the presence of the elements now present in it, we cannot conceive how the formation of a superficial crust was possible.

First. Because of the *agitation of the surface*

by the process of *convection*, to which our attention has been called by Lyell. That tremendous agitation of the primitive ocean, to which Winchell refers, would have been less than a ripple caused by the gentlest zephyr, in comparison with the spouting, out-bursting exhibitions of the heart-force from within the mass of molten matter. And this activity must have continued until the whole mass came near the temperature of solidification.

Secondly. Because of the effect which must have been exerted by the tides. We speak not now of the ocean tides, but of tides in the molten mass itself. It would seem that these must have been of far greater magnitude than the ocean tides now are, and that they must have broken up the incipient crust, which, falling into the mass and subjected to the convulsing agencies of the convectional process, would be broken, crushed, and fused. So we are brought again to the same conclusion, that if the earth *were* once molten it could not, by the simple process of cooling, become solid superficially while remaining fluid internally from retained heat.

CHAPTER X.

TERRESTRIAL CHANGES.

Earthquakes and volcanoes—Molten interior earth—Thickness of the earth's crust—Subterranean lakes of fire—Habitual volcanic action.

DO the advocates of the nebular theory ask, "If the interior of the earth be *not* in a molten condition, how can we account for earthquakes and volcanoes?" We may reply with another question, "If the interior of the earth *be* in a molten condition, with a thin superficial crust, how can we account for earthquakes and volcanoes?"

By the internal tides? Then volcanic eruptions must be greatest in the line of the moon's path, and they must occur regularly twice every day the year round. Moreover, as in the ocean, there are spring tides, caused by the joint influence of the sun and moon; and neap tides, arising from their quadrature; so, also, in the interior molten mass there must be spring tides and neap tides, and we should see their effects in increased volcanic activity. But we do not see *any* of the manifestations of such interior tides. The volcanoes are not situated in any such zone as this hypothesis would require, and their activity is not at all correspondent to the supposition.

But we have also shown that such internal tides would break the crust itself in pieces, and that its permanent formation would be impossible till the interior mass had cooled off to near the temperature of solidification. Then there would remain no interior molten earth, to account for earthquakes and volcanoes. Still, we must not ignore the fact that many geologists do maintain the theory of a central molten earth, and that they by it undertake to account for earthquakes and volcanoes.

Nearly all the elementary works on physical geography and on geology designed for the use of schools, and nearly all the popular treatises on these subjects, teach the theory of an internal molten condition of the earth, and sometimes the volcanic openings are described as the "safety-valves of the globe."

Perhaps we should gratefully contemplate these singular provisions for the world's safety, and just here lay down our pen. But we choose to continue our inquiry. We open one of the elementary text-books of the day, and find that "it is believed by most geologists that the interior of the earth is in a molten state, that the whole earth has been in that condition, and that the crust or solid portion is not more than fifty or one hundred miles thick."—*Tenny's Geology*.

The grounds of this belief of geologists are various, but the most plausible are the observed increase of temperature in mines, and the similar increase of the temperature of the waters of artesian wells, as we go down into the greater depths.

"The sun does not affect the temperature of the earth below the depth of one hundred feet. But for every forty-five or fifty feet of descent below that point the temperature rises about one degree Fahrenheit. If the increase go on at that rate, a point would soon be reached where the heat is sufficient to melt all known substances."—*Tenny*.

Our readers can make their own estimates. Every fifty feet of depth below the first one hundred feet is equal to one degree of heat.

Now iron melts at 2,786 degrees; gold, at 2,590 degrees; zinc, at 680 degrees; lead, at 612 degrees; bismuth, at 540 degrees; sodium, at 200 degrees, etc. How far down must we go to find a heat sufficient to fuse iron? Evidently we must go 100+50×2,786 degrees= 139,400 feet, and that is 26.4 miles. But Sir Isaac Newton has shown that when a metal of low fusibility is mixed with one of high fusibility, the two metals will melt at a lower temperature than either of them would melt at alone. By combining bismuth, lead, and tin, he produced an alloy which melted below two hundred and twelve degrees. We know that silica, and soda, and potash are abundant in the earth, and though silica withstands the heat of the blow-pipe, yet we know that it readily fuses in the glass manufacturer's furnace when mixed with lime, soda, and potash.

We might extend our list of substances, each of which acts as a flux to others, making them less refractory when mixed together. Now we are contemplating a mass of matter in which all the elements are intermixed. We are not at liberty to say the temperature must be raised to the point at which platinum, or silica, or alumina would separately fuse before the mass of mixed elements will be found fused. We shall probably be justified in assuming that at the fusing temperature of iron or gold, the mass of the material of the earth would be fused. Then we should be brought also to the conclusion that the crust of the earth cannot be more than 26.4 miles thick.

Our geologists are apparently startled by their own figures. At least they are considerate of the nerves of the common people, who have no idea how near they are to the great lake of liquid fire. An egg shell is of great thickness when compared with this supposititious terrestrial shell.

But the geologist says the thickness is fifty or one hundred miles, as if fifty were almost one hundred, leaving a slight margin to meet the contingency of any minute error that might have slipped into the calculation.

Before we leave this subject we would remark that the data on which these estimates of the rate of increase of heat are based are too meager to justify a general conclusion. That there is an increase of temperature as we descend into mines is true, and that there is an increase of temperature in water from lower depths is also true; but physicists are by no means agreed as to its cause. It may be chemical; it may be mechanical; it may be proximity to subterranean fires; and yet those fires may be local.

The deepest well of which we know is that at Sperenburg, near Berlin, Prussia. That well, it is said, does not indicate a uniform increase of temperature as we descend. The well is four thousand one hundred and ninety-four feet deep. At the depth of one hundred feet the temperature was 57.2 degrees; at one thousand feet it was 73.8 degrees, an increase of one degree for every 54.2 feet; at the depth of two thousand feet the temperature was 91.4 degrees, an increase of one degree for every 56.8 feet; at the depth of three thousand feet the temperature was 109.4 degrees, an increase of one for every 55.5 feet; and at the depth of four thousand feet the temperature was 118.6 degrees, an increase of one degree for every 108 feet.

It would seem, then, that there is no certain rate of increase of heat as we descend into the earth. It is possible that the next thousand feet would show still less increase. It may be that there is in the solid earth, to the depth of four or five miles, sufficient chemical activity to produce a sensible increase of temperature. It may be that magnetic or electrical conditions exist, which, if known, would elucidate all. All we certainly know is that the increase of temperature is not uniform, nor uniformly accelerated, as we have reason to expect it to be, on the supposition that the whole globe is molten matter, except a thin crust.

We open another elementary text-book of geology, and we read: "The appreciable or ponderable crust of the earth, however, calculating from the astronomical phenomena of precession and nutation, cannot be less than a fourth or a fifth of the earth's radius; that is, it cannot be much less than eight hundred miles."—*Wells's First Prin. Geol.*

The precession of the equinoxes is caused by the attraction of the sun and moon on the equatorial protuberances of the earth. It is evident that the amount of disturbance which would result from these attractions would not be the same if the earth were fluid that they would if the earth were wholly or chiefly solid.

Mr. Hopkins, after carefully estimating the effects of these attractions on the different suppositions, says: "Upon the whole, then, we may venture to assert *that the minimum thickness* of the crust of the globe, which can be deemed consistent with the observed amount of precession, *cannot be less* than one fourth or one fifth of the earth's radius."

Pratt arrived at the same conclusion from an estimation of the crushing force of certain great mountain masses, and Sir William Thompson reached the same conclusion from a consideration of the tides. If, then, we have a central molten earth, we are obliged to conceive of it as separated from the surface by a rocky crust of from eight hundred to one thousand miles in thickness.

We now return to the question, "If the interior of the earth be a molten mass, enveloped by a *thin* shell, how can we account for earthquakes and volcanoes?" Do the phenomena attendant upon earthquakes and volcanoes indicate a molten condition of the *interior* of the earth? They do indicate a molten condition of a *portion* of the earth. But is it a *central* portion? Is it a portion whose perpendicular distance from the point of surface exhibition must be reckoned at a score or two score, or by even hundreds of miles? Do they indicate a common origin, that is, are the phenomena such as could proceed from a common source? Does not each indicate an origin, respectively, in a local subterranean chamber? How extensive the subterranean lakes of fire are we may never know; yet, compared with the globe itself, they are probably small.

How, otherwise, can we account for the fact that volcanoes are so widely separated and so local? The whole world is not volcanic. But there are districts which are now volcanic and have been for ages, and there are other districts which were once volcanic, and are now, and have been for ages, free from volcanic action. If volcanoes originated in the *central* part of the earth, then, whatever be the nature of the forces which produced them, and whatever be the method of their generation, we should expect to find them more generally distributed than they are, unless we refer them to internal tides.

Again, assuming that the earth's crust is fifty miles thick, then what prevents the slender chimneys of the volcanoes becoming clogged and utterly stopped by the ascending column of liquid rocks being cooled and solidified? We do soberly question the possibility of keeping the world's safety-valves open if the molten matter has to be lifted a perpendicular height of fifty miles through the small chimney that a volcano offers for its passage.

But we are compelled to contemplate a still longer chimney by the calculations of Hopkins. It cannot be less than eight hundred miles. Now, while it would tax our credulity to admit the existence of any forces in the central chambers of the earth which could lift a perpendicular column of lava of eight hundred miles, we are even less ready to believe that such a long column could possibly maintain its liquidity.

But there is great difficulty in accounting for the ejection of the lava from so great a depth, and especially from so vast a chamber as the interior of the earth must be if its crust is only fifty, or even one hundred miles thick. We can conceive of a comparatively small subterranean chamber being formed by the changes of the constituent portions of the rocks effected by chemical action; we can conceive of the evolution of heat, the liberation of gases, the melting of rocks, the generation of steam, and the consequent exertion of immense force upon the surrounding mass. And conceiving of the crust above the supposed chamber as being comparatively thin, we can conceive of these forces being intensified to such a degree that they will effect a rupture of the rocks and produce an earthquake or a volcano, or both. But if we refer the earthquake to the same class of forces, and conceive of them as being generated below the crust, whether we suppose that crust to be fifty miles or eight hundred miles thick, then we have an entirely different condition of things. If there be any space at all between the liquid central mass and the solid crust, we shall find it closed on the sides where tides are formed, and open on the sides in quadrature thereto. If the forces that are generated are greater than the upward tidal pressure, they will more than support the crust —provided that they can be confined—and will cause a succession of earthquakes as the earth revolves on its axis, the strain being constantly transferred to that portion which is in quadrature with the tide.

But in any event, if the forces which are supposed to cause the earthquake are gases or steam, and if they be supposed to be generated at the surface of the liquid mass, they will have an immense area over which they must extend before they can exert any lifting or disrupting power, and whatever power they exert must be almost equally exerted over that immense area. We do not see how this class of agencies—steam, gas, etc.—can ever produce a volcanic eruption; that is, how they could, by their pressure on the surface of the molten mass, cause a column of it to ascend through one of these volcanic chimneys, unless it should be in those regions where the internal tides press against the crust; and when we consider how brief a time the tide can last at any given point, we shall see that there would not be time for the upward flow to reach the surface of the earth before the open space would be brought beneath the chimney.

But we are unable to perceive how there could ever be any considerable accumulation of gas or steam beneath the crust under the conditions that are known to exist, for the diurnal rotation would be constantly bringing the open space under the chimneys, and the forces would be constantly escaping. A steam boiler with a hundred leaks, though they were no larger than a hair, would be regarded as an inefficient motor agency. We cannot see how the escape of the forces could be avoided. Every fracture of the crust, as well as every old opening, would allow them to escape. How, then, could they accumulate so as to push up even a fifty-mile column of molten rock, and display all the activities of actual eruptions.

Volcanic energies are known to increase in the same locality for days and weeks, and then to culminate in grand eruptions, followed by seasons of quiet. How can such local paroxysms be reconciled with the theory of an internal liquid mass and an outer crust?

But having proceeded thus far on the presumption that there might be a generation of steam in the interior of the earth, *we now call in question the possibility of such generation.* Winchell says: "Consider that in the present condition of our globe the water and air must be unable to penetrate more than one fiftieth the distance to the earth's center. Percolating downward through the rocks, the water soon reaches a temperature which dissipates it into vapor, and returns it toward the surface to be recondensed."

One fiftieth the distance to the earth's center is about eighty miles. That is thirty miles further than many geologists allow for the thickness of the earth's crust. Let us make an estimate on the assumption that the temperature increases one degree for every fifty feet of descent. At the depth of one hundred feet the temperature averages about fifty-eight degrees. At two hundred and twelve degrees water is converted to vapor. At four hundred and fifty-six degrees steam has a tension equal to thirty atmospheres. At this tension is it likely to penetrate farther into the rocky depths? Let us suppose that at four hundred and fifty-six degrees of temperature the descent of water will be arrested. What depth has it reached? $456° - 58° = 398°$. And

398°×50 feet=19,900 feet. Add 100 feet, at which depth the average temperature is about 58 degrees, and we have 20,000 feet. And 20,000 feet are only about 3.8 miles. One has only to look at these figures to see how loosely a theorist will sometimes express himself on a scientific subject.

Certainly, if we grant the premises—to wit, that for every fifty feet of descent the temperature rises one degree—we must conclude that water will be converted into steam at the depth of seven thousand eight hundred feet, and that at the depth of 3.8 miles the steam, if it could penetrate so far, would have a tension of thirty atmospheres.

We conclude that such a temperature would exclude it—if the reasoning of Winchell on this point be correct—and that water, therefore, could not penetrate the earth below that depth. But this, instead of being one fiftieth is only about one thousandth part of the distance to the center of the earth. But the heat which is supposed to exist *below* the earth's crust is many times as great as that which produces steam of the tension of thirty atmospheres. It is a heat of fusion for all known substances. And before reaching the fusing point the rocks must be conceived to be at red heat. Water certainly would not "percolate" long through red-hot rocks. How, then, can steam ever be generated *below* the earth's crust?

If the volcanoes have their origin in the central molten globe, how can we account for the different habitual behavior of different volcanoes?

There is, in many of the existing volcanoes, what may be called *characteristic behavior?* Stromboli, which so long ago as the time of Homer received honorable mention, is a kind of restless, fussy volcano, always active, but never remarkably so. Ashes and vapor ascend out of its crater daily, and its eruptions occur periodically at intervals of three to five months. Rancagua, in Chili, is another active, but moderate, volcano. Vesuvius has long seasons of great tranquillity, followed by tremendous subterranean convulsions and overwhelming discharges of lava and ashes. Etna, in these respects, resembles Vesuvius. Hecla is a volcano of stupendous energy. It sometimes rests for a period of years; then it gathers its forces, wraps itself in flames, and energizes marvelously for years, until it seems to be exhausted with the fury of its own rage, and it settles down again into quiet. Mauna Loa has the singular habit of running over in a very quiet manner, and sending great rivers of liquid lava to the sea with very little disturbance to the land. While other volcanoes usually announce the approach of their great eruptions by great quakings and subterranean mutterings, Mauna Loa scarcely sounds a note of warning.

These are marked distinctive characteristics of these different volcanoes. They indicate differences in their origin. If we refer them to the different constituents of the rocks from which they arise, we have an assigned cause, which is in harmony with their behavior. If we refer them to the central liquid earth, as the *common* source of all volcanoes, we are unable to reconcile their behavior with our supposition. The volcanic district of which Mauna Loa is the center is the theater of volcanic action so singular that we cannot forbear to extend our examination of it, with direct reference to the theories we are discussing.

Hawaii is the largest of the Sandwich Islands. Mauna Loa is a volcanic mountain in the southern part of the island. It is about fourteen thousand feet high. Since it became known to the civilized world a number of eruptions have occurred. In 1843, during an eruption, a rent twenty-five miles long was made in the mountain. In 1852 another eruption took place, during which the liquid lava rose to near the top of the crater and flowed out at a small opening. Meanwhile the pressure of the mighty column caused a break of great magnitude, about four thousand feet lower down, and here it threw up a jet of lava one thousand feet in diameter to a height of seven hundred feet. Another eruption in 1855 continued during several months to send forth a river of lava, which extended to a distance of sixty-five miles, and was three to five miles wide. Again, in 1859, on the night of January 23, without warning, it vomited forth its liquid fires so abundantly that they ran twenty-five miles during the night. Jets of liquid fire were projected upward to the height of one thousand five hundred feet. Reaching the sea, at a distance of forty miles, the volcanic river extended two miles into the water. All these eruptions have been attended with breaks in the mountain some distance below the summit, so great was the force exerted by the higher column of molten lava on the side of the mountain.

About sixteen miles from Mauna Loa, at an elevation of only four thousand feet above the level of the sea, is Kilauea, the most remarkable crater in the world. Kilauea is an immense depression, one thousand feet deep, three miles long, and about one mile wide. In the bottom of this immense crater are smaller craters of different elevations, in which the volcanic action is always to be seen in pools and lakes of lava. Standing on the brink of the chasm the spectator beholds the lava in one of these pools rising to the height of one hundred and fifty feet or more, while in another it may descend one hundred feet or more. Perhaps one of them will be spouting furiously while another will be quiet and placid. This great crater has also sent forth its rivers of molten rocks. Mr. Ellis visited it in 1823, and he describes two of the lava pools at the bottom, the largest of which he says was one thousand one hundred and ninety yards long. During that year there was an eruption from Kilauea of such magnitude that the lava stream, where it entered the sea, was four or five miles wide.

Another eruption took place in 1832, and another in 1840. Of this eruption Mr. Coan, an American missionary to the Sandwich Islanders, gives an interesting description:—

"Imagine to yourself a river of fused materials of the breadth and depth of Niagara, and of a gory red, falling in one emblazoned sheet, one raging torrent, into the ocean! The atmosphere in all directions was filled with ashes, spray, and gases, while the burning lava, as it fell into the water, was shivered into millions of minute particles, and, being thrown back into the air, fell in showers of sand on all the surrounding country.

"The coast was extended into the sea a quarter of a mile. Three hills of scoria and sand were also formed in the sea, the lowest about two hundred and the highest about three hundred feet high. For three weeks this terrific river disgorged itself into the sea with little abatement. The waters were heated for twenty miles along the coast, and multitudes of fishes were killed. The breadth of the stream where it fell into the sea is about half a mile, but inland it varies from one to four miles in width, conforming, like a river, to the face of the country over which it flowed. The depth varies from ten feet to two hundred, according to the inequalities over which it passed. The whole course of the stream, from Kilauea to the sea, is about forty miles."

We have thus given, as briefly as possible, an account of these two most singular craters and their action. But the most remarkable fact is yet to be mentioned. That fact is that these two craters seem never to be in sympathy with each other. Mauna Loa may be sending forth a vast river of lava from a height of fourteen thousand feet, and Kilauea will repose as quietly as if no great event were transpiring.

While the great river runs from Mauna Loa we look to see the larger and lower crater of Kilauea fill up with lava and run over. And we look for it the more confidently when we behold the pressure of the vast column of lava in Loa affecting great breaks in the mountain far down its sides. But we look in vain. And we involuntarily ask, "Are these two craters, thus near each other, connected? Are they both outlets of the same interior ocean?"

Why, then, does not the liquid lava rise equally in both? How can a column fourteen thousand feet high exist in connection with an opening only four thousand feet high, and yet not flow out at that lower opening at all? How is it that while a stream of lava flows from near that elevated summit, the pools of Kilauea only vibrate vertically or spout as they ordinarily do?

All fluids seek an equilibrium. This is not less true of iron and other metals when melted than it is of water. And we take advantage of this principle or law of fluids to convert pig-iron into castings of various forms. Were it not for this law, all cast forms would be impossible. Whenever, then, a molten liquid mass, of whatever element, rising in a duct, finds a lateral opening sufficient for its volume, it will follow the lateral outlet in preference to going higher. That it would do this in these Hawaian craters if the chimneys were connected is evident from the fact that the very mountain mass of Loa is burst open by the immense pressure, and the lava does make its escape several thousand feet below the summit at every eruption. Now let it be assumed that the huge duct leading from the central earth to Mauna Loa divides at some point in the depths, something as indicated in the following figure:—

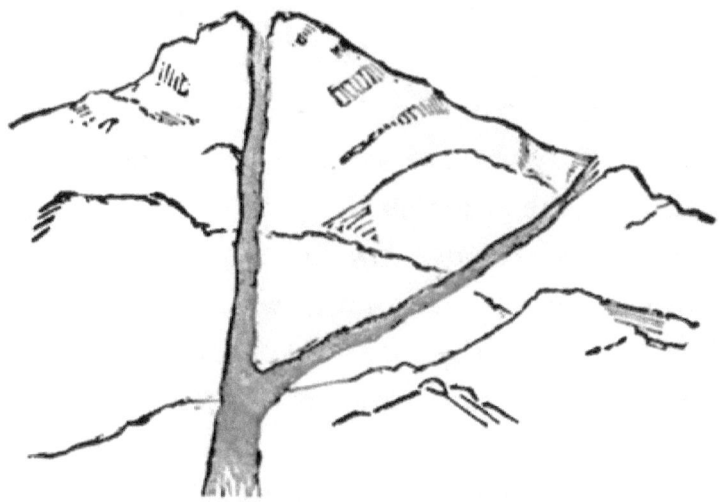

We can conceive that in the formation of the volcano, in the upheaving of the mountain, the solid crust would be so broken as to afford two or more openings several miles apart, and that these openings should be in communication with each other, and so long as these openings were on the same level, they would equally answer as outlets for the liquid lava which should rise to the surface and seek an outlet.

But it is insupposable that the molten matter would follow one volcanic chimney only when there were two equally eligible ones meeting at a point far below the place of discharge. Rising in either, the law of equilibrium would cause it to rise equally in the other.

If, then, two craters, of unequal altitude, be connected with the same main chimney, we shall find the *lower crater active, in all cases, before the higher one can be.*

But here is one crater which is fourteen thousand feet high, and another crater, only sixteen miles away, which is only four thousand feet high. And this lower crater always exhibits some degree of activity. Its lakes and pools of lava are always liquid and in motion, thus showing, that wherever the origin of their volcanic activity may be, between it and these pools and lakes the communication is constant, and the intermediate chimney is always filled with liquid lava. The rising and falling of the pools show that there is no impediment to the freedom of its vertical movements, and therefore, however long the column may be, it moves freely throughout its whole extent. There is nothing, then, to hinder the higher column from exerting the whole force of its pressure on the lower, if they be united at *any* point. How tremendous must that pressure be! Moreover, the history of these two craters shows that wherever the source of their respective streams of lava may be, the opening to the two craters are ample, for the outpourings have been immense. Those great *rivers* of lava, of which we have just given an account, declare how ample were the openings through which they came from the depths.

In view of these facts we venture the suggestion that these great craters cannot be connected at all. They have not a common origin. As two separate districts not remote from each other may be underlaid by one great coal field, as many different shafts may be sunk, and each district extensively undermined and its treasures of coal brought to the surface, so we may conceive of the same character of rocks to underlie vast areas, and the conditions necessary to chemical action therein to be gradually prepared by the forces that are ever operating among elements and masses; then we shall have the chemical reactions, the evolution of heat, the increase of chemical action, and the melting of the rocks. If water be present in quantities more than sufficient to promote the chemical action, it may be converted into steam; and if the heat be sufficient to fuse metals the steam must be superheated, and its expansive power would be such as to cause fractures in the walls of the concavity, which the steam and gases must immediately penetrate, thus extending the theater of chemical action. And thus we can conceive how the upper portion of the rocky structure may be lifted, and the active forces advanced, until an opening to the surface is effected. It would, perhaps, be presumptuous to say that this probably is the mode in which volcanoes have originated. But certainly this seems more nearly to satisfy the rational conditions of their formation than the theory of a central origin. And it may be remarked that if we find it impossible to reconcile the action of one volcano to the theory of central origin—if we can account for it on other principles—then that central molten globe ceases to be a theoretical necessity, and it vanishes out of cosmical history as one of a congeries of assumptions.

The characteristic behavior of various volcanoes is equally against that theory which assigns, as their cause, the constant contraction or shrinking of the earth's crust.

There is another set of facts which we ought to take into account in this discussion. Volcanic regions are generally near the sea or other body of water. Between the sea and that subterranean cavity in which the volcanic materials are prepared there is evidently some sort of communication, so that the waters percolating through the rocks or following minute channels furnish the moisture which is requisite for the production of chemical activity and the supply of the steam force which is brought into play at the time of an eruption. It is known, also, that in volcanic districts subterranean lakes do exist, which are filled with fishes. Sometimes the separating walls are broken down, and the waters of such a lake are precipitated into the volcanic chamber, and the fish are thrown out at the crater during an eruption, the activity of which is enhanced by the waters. " So great a quantity of these fish were ejected from the volcano of Imbabura in 1691, that fevers, which prevailed at the period, were attributed to the effluvia arising from the putrid animal matter."—*Lyell.*

Professor Ehrenberg has found that "volcanic products abound with the flinty shells of minute microscopic animals." If this be true, it would imply that the lava was once sedimentary rock, in which such minute animals were imbedded, and it would utterly forbid the supposition that it came from a primitive molten interior mass. For surely no one will claim that there is any animal life in that central globe of fire.

CHAPTER XI.

THE MOON.

Favorably situated for telescopic observation—Has the moon an atmosphere?—Or water?—Shape of the moon—Is the moon a frozen-up world?

NEAREST of the heavenly bodies; almost equal in apparent magnitude to the sun; shining with pure, steady, and serene light; waxing and waning with undeviating regularity, the moon is one of the most interesting objects of nocturnal observation. Its mean distance from the earth is at present estimated to be about 238,800 miles. Its diameter is 2,162.3 miles. Its entire surface, therefore, is about 14,500,000 square miles. So near to us, is it strange that it has been the subject of interminable conjecture and speculation? Its nearness excites the more persistent examination, because it inspires the greatest hopes of arriving at certain knowledge. These hopes have been encouraged by another fact. The same hemisphere of the moon is always turned toward the earth. So the telescopic observer is able to fix his attention on any given spot, and he knows that the axial rotation of the moon is not going to slip that spot out of his view immediately. So long as the moon itself is in view the spot he is examining will remain in view.

There is, however, one circumstance that diminishes our satisfaction with this situation of things. There is a large area upon the moon's surface that is absolutely unobservable by us. The total area brought into view, including that exposed by the moon's librations, does not exceed three fifths of the whole surface.

Astronomers have long held that there was but little, if any, atmosphere upon the moon. They thought, however, that they detected the existence of extended seas, and lunar maps were made on which the seas were shown, with names to distinguish them. When we reflect that there was supposed to be no atmosphere, and consequently there could be no wild lunar storms, we are not surprised to find among the seas a *Mare Tranquillitatis* and a *Mare Serenitatis.*

That the moon has no atmosphere has been inferred from the fact that a planet or star in occultation with the moon seemed to pass out of sight instantly, as it would not do if there were an atmosphere to refract its light. Airy has shown that if there be a lunar atmosphere its refractive power cannot exceed $\frac{1}{2,000}$ part of that of the atmosphere of the earth.

Sir William Herschell gave this subject special attention. On the 5th of September, 1793, during a solar eclipse, he observed with great care the acute horn resulting from the intersection of the limbs of the sun and the moon. "His deduction, from his observations, was, that if there had been a deviation of one second, caused by the refraction of the solar light by a lunar atmosphere, it would not have escaped him."

Spectrum analysis has also been directed to the determination of this question. Fraunhofer, Brewster, Huggins, Gladstone, Miller, Jansen, and others have respectively made it the subject of study. "From the entire absence of any special absorption lines," Schellen says, "it must be concluded that there is no atmosphere in the moon."

With the conviction that the moon is destitute of an atmosphere, there has also come a general conviction that there are no bodies of water on the moon, and those areas, which were formerly supposed to be seas, are now supposed to be sandy plains. Some think that they retain the marks of former sea bottoms; some see in them the evidences of aerial action, and they fancy that there once existed both air and water on the moon. Some account for the disappearance of the water by supposing that the volcanic agencies produced such immense subterraneous caverns that the waters all drained off into them; but Winchell supposes the rocks to have literally absorbed them, together with the atmosphere.

We are not writing a lunar history, and therefore it is all one to us whether there be a lunar atmosphere and lunar seas or not. We have no theory that requires the assumption that they did once exist, and which, if they are found *not* to exist at the present time, must account for their disappearance.

But the moon is, in the nebular theory, a representative body. It represents the "Lunar Stage," that is, the stage of final refrigeration, and what the moon now *is*, that the earth, the planets, and the sun are destined to become.

Leaving for a moment the question of the physical condition of the moon as an unsettled question, which it is, we remark that the moon performs an important office in its effects on terrestrial economy. Perhaps no one can appreciate at its real value the benefit to all terrestrial life of that tidal movement whose efficient cause is the lunar attraction.

But to return, the advocates of the nebular theory point us to evidences of great volcanic activity on the moon during some periods of its history. And no one can deny that there is the appearance on the hither hemisphere of the moon of such activity. Steep precipices; lofty rocky mountains, unrelieved by vegetation; extensive parks of barren sand, surrounded by rugged ridges of naked rocks; great cavities, not unlike some of the extinct craters of the earth, combine to make upon us the impression that we have before us a scene of absolute desolation.

But no volcanoes are found at present in action. Sir William Herschell thought at one time that he had seen an eruption of a lunar volcano, but Arago expresses strong doubts of the reality of the eruption. We think it quite probable that no active volcano exists on the hither side of the moon. Here, now, are three facts—at least they are supposed to be facts: there is no atmosphere in the moon, there is no water in the moon, there is no volcanic activity in the moon.

From these three facts the nebular theory is supposed to have strong confirmation, and the lunar history is readily written as follows:—

The moon was detached from the earth while it was an aeriform body. Being a very small body it rapidly cooled off and contracted, and its elements combined; it became liquid, and a crust was formed upon it; and there was an atmosphere; and there were seas; and subsequently there were great convulsions; the internal fires generated forces that lifted portions of the crust, or broke through as volcanoes. All these changes occurred with great rapidity compared with the corresponding changes in the earth, because the moon is so small. At length the lunar fires burned quite out, the volcanic activity ceased. At one time there was life on the moon. The lunar seas were full of lunar fishes, the lunar air was cleft by wings of lunar birds, the lunar forests were thronged by lunar beasts. Then, too, some higher type of being, answering to that of man on the earth, reigned over all the lunar realms. But that was in the long, long ago.

The historic periods succeeded each other rapidly. The internal fires were spent. The whole mass became solid. The solid structure became gradually chilled. The rocks eagerly drank up the water, and, still unsatisfied, absorbed the atmosphere, and now the heat is quite exhausted. All life has become extinct. The moon is a frozen world, and it hangs in the heavens an impressive example of a *single stage* of planetary history.

As the rings of Saturn were an example and a demonstration of the ring stage of planetary evolution, so the frozen-up moon is an example and a demonstration of planetary congelation; and it follows that all planetary history begins in fire-mist, passes through successive stages of cooling, contracting, solidifying, convulsing, renewing, etc., until the end shall come in a universal waste of frozen, desolate, wandering spheres, wrapped in the darkness of eternal night, the sun itself shrunken and frozen.

Such may be the end foreshadowed. And it is not the province of true science to shed tears over the foreseen catastrophe. It is only her province to take the facts of history, as the great plan of nature is unfolded, and interpret them on known natural principles. And yet the generalizations of science should not be too precipitate. Moderation and self-distrust are as likely to be needed here as in any sphere of scientific inquiry. What we *know*, not what we imagine or what we conjecture, should be the basis of our generalization. Do we *know* enough about the moon to pronounce positively as to its physical condition? Do we know that it is frozen up? Do we know that there is neither air nor water on the moon? True, we see no signs of air on the hither hemisphere. No clouds float across its disk. And both the telescope and the spectroscope fail to find any indications of an atmosphere. But let us not forget that there are about six millions of square miles of lunar surface that we have not examined, and cannot examine with the telescope or spectroscope. Who can tell what is there out of sight? Is there any means by which we can arrive at the probabilities in the case? It may be said that the probabilities are just what the general *opinion* of scientists is, and the general opinion is that there is no atmosphere and no water on the moon.

And there is weight in this fact, for it is to be presumed that scientists will not commit themselves to an opinion which has not a high degree of probability. But it will not be considered disrespectful to re-open the question. The inaccessibility of the farther lunar hemisphere is itself a factor to be considered in the solution of this problem. Why can we not observe that hemisphere? Why is it always turned away from us? Evidently because the moon is not balanced upon its own center. The hemisphere of greater density is toward the earth, and the earth holds it there, (not exactly steadily, for it has its librations,) and it cannot change its relations.

The hemisphere of lesser density, then, is out of sight. Now let us consider the effect of the moon's motion on the moon's form. We agree that the form of each of the planetary bodies is affected by its axial rotation. The effect on the earth has been to give it an oblateness of $\frac{1}{289}$; on Mars, to give it an oblateness of $\frac{1}{50}$; on Jupiter, to give it an oblateness of $\frac{1}{17}$; and on Saturn, to give it an oblateness of $\frac{1}{10}$. But is any such effect possible to the moon? We venture to express the conviction that it is not. The moon, then, cannot be an oblate spheroid.

Why do we come to this conclusion? Because of the moon's diurnal motion. The moon does not revolve upon its own axis as the earth does and as other planets do. The earth is the center of its diurnal rotation. If an artificial globe be firmly fixed to the end of an arm which moves around a fixed point, it will fairly represent the moon's motion. Is there any centrifugal force generated? Yes. What effect will it have on the moon? It will cause it to tend to fly off *bodily* from the center. Will it affect its form? If it does, it must raise its *outer hemisphere*, and give to the body an oval or ovate form. The form, we think, must be ovate. If any fluid matter does exist on the moon, this motion of the body must necessarily throw it to or toward the other side. We are not certain that this would not be the case if we should consider the moon a solid body in the sense in which the crust of the earth is a solid body. For in this solid crust are cavities, and seams, and channels, in which water may be, and through which it may pass.

Suppose, then, that the whole earth be thus solid, and that its axial rotation be arrested, and it go on in its orbit as usual. Would not all the oceans be piled up on one side, and that the side opposite to the sun? And all the water that was land-locked, so that it could not pass *over*, would gradually strain *through* to, or toward, that other side. Take a sponge and attach it to a revolving arm—will not the moisture all collect at that side which is most distant from the center of rotation, provided the rotation be sufficiently rapid? Just so, if there be any atmosphere and any water on the moon, the effect of this known motion of the moon must be to gather all the surface-water and most of the air to that farther side which is inaccessible to our observation. We say *most of the air*, because we conceive that the expansibility of air would probably cause it to extend over the whole surface, but not of equal depths.

This supposition as to the waters of the moon does not exclude the possibility of volcanic action on the hither lunar hemisphere. If volcanoes originate in the chemical changes which may take place in the rocks, such changes may be supposed to have been in progress for ages, and the absence of such agencies as are so powerful on the earth in modifying the *surface appearance* (the aqueous and aerial agencies) would have the effect to leave the volcanic chasms, and ridges, and rents just as the volcanic action itself shaped them, and we, who look down into the awful depths of those craters, behold them just as they were left by the receding fires.

On the earth heat, cold, moisture, and the force of the wind, destroy the original ruggedness of terrestrial mountains. In the absence of water and air the alternations of temperature and cold would affect them but slightly.

It may be said that these thoughts touching a possible condition of the moon are but speculative. True; and so, too, the theory which represents the moon as "a fossil world, an ancient cinder," is but a speculative theory.

We do not *know* that one hemisphere of the moon has water on its surface, but we know that with the moon's known diurnal motion, if there be any water on the moon, it would find that side and would stay there. And inasmuch as that is the case, the blistered, waterless, and airless aspects of the hither hemisphere are no ground at all for the conclusion that the oceans and atmosphere of the moon are sucked up by the rocks, and have totally disappeared from the lunar surface. It certainly is not demonstrable that the moon is a frozen-up world, having a temperature like that which prevails at the top of the Himalayas and the Alps. Nor is it demonstrable that it is a habitable world. Our consideration of its aspects and its motions leads us to the conclusion that it *may be habitable*, but if so it is only in one hemisphere, and that the hemisphere we are unable to observe. According to very recent thermometrical experiments the moon actually does emit heat in quantities sufficient to produce sensible effects at the distance of the earth. Fourteen and a half days of unclouded sunshine on the hither hemisphere of the moon, it is now estimated, produces in it an average temperature of boiling water. Certainly it is not a reliable subject from which to deduce that portion of the cosmical history which is called "the lunar stage," or stage of final refrigeration. Fourteen and a half days of continual sunshine would also cause the waters of the farther hemisphere to evaporate rapidly, and we can imagine dense clouds forming and protecting that hemisphere from the heat of the long-continued day, and mitigating the rigors of an equally protracted night.

Since penning the foregoing we have, by a happy chance, opened the "Annual of Scientific Discovery," for 1858, to the following interesting account of the occultation of Jupiter by the moon, which occurred on the 2d of January, 1857. We quote a portion only of the article:—

"But the most interesting fact yet remains to be told. The bright border of the moon at this time crossed the soft green face of the planet, not with a clear, sharply-cut outline, like that which had been presented as the disc, passed into concealment; it was fringed by a streak or band of graduated shadow, commencing at the moon's edge as a deep-black line, and being then stippled off outwardly until it dissolved away in the green light of the planet's face. This shade-band was about a tenth part of the planet's disc broad, and of equal breadth from end to end. Mr. Lassell described it as offering to his practiced eye precisely the same appearance the obscure ring of Saturn presents to a higher magnifying power where that appendage crosses in front of the body of the Saturnian sphere. There could be no mistake concerning the actual existence of this curious and unexpected apparition. It was independently noticed and described by at least six trustworthy observers, and the descriptions of it, given by each of these, corresponded with the minutest accuracy. The shadow was seen and described by Mr. Lassell, at Liverpool; by the Rev. Professor Challis, at the Observatory at Cambridge; by the Rev. W. R. Dawes, at Wateringbury; by Dr. Mann and Captain Swingburne, at Ventnor; and by Mr. William Simms, at Carshalton. It therefore only needs that the unusual presence should be accounted for; the handwriting being there, the question remains to be answered, 'Can its interpretation be found?' Can science read the meaning of this shadow-fringe inscription? Are there minds that can fathom, as well as eyes that could catch, this signal hint thrown out by Jupiter at the instant of its emergence from its forced concealment behind the moon?

"It was Mr. Dawes's impression, on the instant, that the mysterious shadow was simply an optical spectrum, a deep, blue fringe to the light haze caused by the object-glass of his telescope having been accidentally over-corrected for one of the irregularities incident to chromatic refraction. This notion, of course, became altogether untenable so soon as it was known that the same appearance had been noted by other telescopes in which the same incidental imperfection had had no place. All felt that the shadow could not be referred to a regular atmospheric investment of the moon's solid sphere, because, under such circumstances, the streak should have always been seen when the rim of the moon rested in a similar way across a planetary disc.

"The sagacious Plumian, professor of astronomy at Cambridge, Professor Challis, seems to have been the first to hit upon the true interpretation of the riddle. The indefatigable star-seer has long suspected that the broad, dark patches of the lunar surface—the seas of the old selenographists—are really shallow basins, filled with a sediment of vapor which has settled down into those depressions; in other words, he conceived that there are fog seas, although there are no water seas, in the moon. The general surface and higher projections of the lunar spheroid are altogether uncovered and bare; but vapors and mists have rolled down into the lower regions in sufficient quantities to fill up the basin-like hollows exactly as water has gravitated into the beds of the terrestrial oceans. The professor, using the high powers of the magnificent telescope furnished to the Cambridge Observatory by the munificence of the late Duke of Northumberland, was able to satisfy himself that the planet actually did come out from behind a widely-gaping hollow of the moon's surface at the bottom of a lunar fog sea, seen edgewise, so to speak. If a shallow basin extended for some distance round the curvature of the lunar spheroid, and if it were filled up with vapor, that vapor would rest at a fixed level, exactly after the manner of a collection of liquid, and such fixed level would be concentric with the general spheroidal curvature of the satellite. Under such an arrangement there would, therefore, necessarily be a bulging protuberance of the vapor-surface through which a remote luminary might be seen when it rested in the requisite position. This, then, is Professor Challis's understanding of Jupiter's hint. The moon has fog seas upon her surface, and the band of shadow visible upon the face of Jupiter, as the planet came out from behind the earth's satellite, was a thin upper slice of one of those fog seas seen by the favorable accident of the planet's light shining for the instant from beyond."

We reproduce this for this purpose only, to show by it how little ground there is to pronounce dogmatically, as Professor Winchell does, that "the moon *is* a fossil world, an ancient cinder," etc., exemplifying an extreme state of *refrigeration* to which all planetary bodies and the sun itself are finally to come.

So far as our knowledge of that satellite goes, it authorizes no such conclusion.

CHAPTER XII.

THE SUN.

Its volume—Density—Temperature—Relation to the planets—Nebular theory applied to the sun—Material constituents—Origin of the Sun's heat—Theory of Helmholtz—Theory of Mayer—Views of Winchell.

THE sun is in all respects the most important body in the solar system. We have given it some general consideration, but it demands more particular and extended examination. We now propose to group together the principal facts that are known respecting this great luminary, and then proceed to an examination of the theoretical inferences drawn from these facts.

The magnitude of the sun is amazing. Taking the volume of the earth as unity, that of the sun is about one million two hundred and fifty thousand. Conceive of the sun as a hollow sphere, with the earth in its center, then the moon might revolve around the earth at its present distance, midway between the earth and the solar shell. Were all the planets united in one body, without any change of density, the sun would equal five hundred such bodies. But if all the planetary bodies could be reduced to a common density, the density of the sun itself, and united in one body, then the sun would equal seven hundred such bodies.

Vast as the magnitude of the sun is, however, it would require *three hundred and forty billions* of such magnitudes to equal that of the original cosmical mass of the nebular theory at the period when Neptune was separated from the parent mass; and we shall be prepared by this fact to contemplate the sun's present magnitude without extravagant emotions. The sun is a self-luminous body, and is the source of light and heat to the entire planetary system. The physical constitution of the sun has been the subject of infinite speculation. That it is a material body, having a specific gravity about one fourth that of the earth, that its gravitative force acts on all planetary matter, and that it binds the planets and satellites and asteroids together in one great system, are facts which have long been established. And it was only natural to conjecture that the material elements of the sun and the material elements of the planets were as kindred in character as were the forces that were known to be active between them.

Men who have reflected were not, therefore, startled into inordinate raptures when that wonderful little instrument, the spectroscope, announced positively and authoritatively that the sun surely contains many of the very same elements contained by the earth. This is only what men have believed to be true for ages. There may be elements in the earth yet unknown to science; and there may be elements in the sun that are not present in the earth; and there may be elements in the stars that are not in either the sun or the earth, nor yet in any of the planets. Certain it is that there are *spectra* which the most eminent and skillful spectroscopists are unable to refer to any known element.

But the majority of the elements may be common to *all* suns and planets, the quantities of each being distributed with reference to the office which each body has to perform in the great system of nature. The physical constitution and condition of the sun, therefore, may be presumed to be exactly what its relation to all the planetary bodies requires. Between the sun and those bodies are vast spaces, yet not so vast as at all to embarrass the force by which they are bound together, or to hinder the efficiency of that solar influence which enlightens and warms them. Such reflections, though concurred in by the physicist and astronomer, do not satisfy them. They would like to know the exact structure of the sun, the condition of its matter, the nature of the solar spots, the origin of its light. Why is the sun self-luminous? How does it generate its heat? A thousand questions have been raised, and men have been ready with answers. And yet the questions are as far from being wholly satisfied as ever.

So long ago as 1769 Dr. Wilson, of Glasgow, suggested that the sun might be an opaque body, surrounded by a luminous atmosphere. Sir William Herschell, in 1795, declared himself convinced that the light-giving substance of the sun was neither liquid nor elastic fluid, but something analogous to our clouds, and that it floated in the transparent atmosphere of that luminary. He conceived that there were two atmospheres, endowed with separate and independent motions. The solar spots were openings in the luminous atmosphere, through which the dark body of the sun could be seen. Sir David Brewster thought that the non-luminous rays that are found in solar light might have been emitted by the dark body of the sun, and the luminous rays have been emitted by the luminous matter. "With this hypothesis," says Sir David, "we could readily explain why it is hottest when there are most spots, because the heat of the nucleus would then reach us without having been weakened by the atmosphere that it usually has to traverse." But so far as we know, it is not "hottest when there are most spots."

Other astronomers have suggested the existence of a third atmosphere, non-luminous and transparent, as indicated by the diminished brightness of the sun's disk toward the edges. In our times the solar light serves the cause of science in ways of which the ancients did not so much as dream. Photography assists the celestial explorer by catching the image of the celestial body, and fixing it for his deliberate examination. Thus the solar spots and protuberances have been subjected to a scrutiny which was impossible to simple telescopic observation.

The spectroscope, also, has greatly enlarged the boundaries of our knowledge of solar affairs, although it must be confessed that distinguished spectroscopists are not fully agreed respecting the constitution of the sun. Kirchhoff's theory is, however, generally accepted. We take the liberty to quote the following from Schellen :—

"According to Kirchhoff the sun consists of a *solid* or *partially liquid* nucleus in the highest state of incandescence, which emits, like all incandescent bodies, every possible kind of light, and, therefore, would of itself give a *continuous* spectrum without any dark lines. This incandescent central nucleus is surrounded by an atmosphere of lower temperature, containing, on account of the extreme heat of the nucleus, the vapors of many of the substances of which this body is composed. The rays of light, therefore, emitted by the nucleus, must pass through this atmosphere before reaching the earth, and each vapor extinguishes from the white light those rays which it would itself emit in a glowing state. Now it is found, when the sun's light is analyzed by a prism, that a multitude of rays are extinguished, and just those rays which would be emitted by the vapors of sodium, iron, calcium, magnesium, etc., were they made self-luminous; consequently the vapors of the following substances, sodium, iron, potassium, calcium, barium, magnesium, manganese, titanium, chromium, nickel, cobalt, hydrogen, and, probably, also zinc, copper, and gold, must exist in the solar atmosphere, and these metals must also be present to a considerable extent in the body of the sun."

Kirchhoff explains the solar spots on the supposition that they are cloud-like masses of condensed vapor floating in the solar atmosphere, and intercepting the rays of light that proceed from the incandescent nucleus.

Faye, on the other hand, supposes the actual nucleus of the sun to be a non-luminous globe of gas, and the solar spots to be huge rents or openings through the luminous envelope, which is called the *photosphere*.

Here are three theories of the solar constitution. Could we believe with Wilson and Herschell, we might imagine the sun a very delightful residence; its dark central body variegated by mountains and valleys, oceans, seas, lakes, and rivers, continents and islands, in infinite variety; with an equable and constant climate, no tropical heats and polar frosts, but a uniformly pleasant and fruitful season, continuing forever; no night, but one unchanging day, while its luminous atmosphere, thousands of miles away, filters its light and heat down through the lower atmosphere upon the whole solar body alike.

But Kirchhoff dispels the happy illusion, and turns our continents into white-hot liquids or solids, while Faye turns the solids and liquids into gas. We will be excused from a residence in the sun, if you please.

Later experiments than those upon which Kirchhoff based his theory, have shown that conditions of temperature *and pressure* may exist under which gases will give unbroken *spectra*, just as incandescent solids and liquids do; and so *it may be* that the light transmitted from the sun is not from a solid or liquid incandescent body.

That distinguished Italian spectroscopist, Sechi, thinks that there exists *aqueous vapor* in the vicinity of the large spots.

In 1868 the French astronomer, Janssen, while watching the total eclipse of the sun from a station in India, noticed that the solar *prominences* gave a spectrum of *three bright lines*, indicating that the prominences were vast columns of incandescent hydrogen.

Lockyer, in England, had already noticed the same phenomenon without the eclipse. He gives the following views, deduced from his observations: " Now these again are facts which bear upon the sun's condition in a very great degree; indeed, they lead us necessarily to several important modifications of the received theory of the physical constitution of our central luminary; the theory which we owe to Kirchhoff, who based it upon his examination of the solar spectrum. According to his idea the photosphere itself is either solid or liquid, and is surrounded by an extensive non-luminous atmosphere, composed of gases and the vapors of the substances incandescent in the photosphere.

" Kirchhoff's idea demands dense vapors

far above where we have found hydrogen alone, and that very rare. So that we must consider that the absorption, to which the reversal of the spectrum and the Fraunhofer lines are due, takes place in the photosphere itself, or extremely near to it, instead of in an extensive outer absorbing atmosphere; so that we may say that the photosphere, plus the chromosphere, is the real atmosphere of the sun, and that the sun itself is in such a state of fervid heat that the outer border of its atmosphere, that is, the chromosphere, is in a state of incandescence."

Professor Young, probably the most distinguished spectroscopist of America, has submitted another theory. He supposes the existence of a liquid solar crust, which restrains the gases for a time, after which they break through in jets. M. Soret finds, with Lockyer, that the higher atmosphere of the sun consists of nothing but hydrogen. This certainly is a very peculiar condition. Another circumstance seems to us most strange, if we can trust the announcements of the spectroscope. "The spectra of the metals, silver, mercury, antimony, arsenic, tin, lead, cadmium, strontium, and lithium, show no coincidence with the Fraunhofer lines, and this is also the case with the two non-metallic substances, silicen and oxygen."—*Schellen.*

Is there, then, no silver, no mercury, no oxygen in the sun? So much fire and no oxygen! No combustion!

No other single element plays so important a part in the terrestrial economy as oxygen. No other has so wide a range of affinity. All the elements combine with it, unless fluorine be an exception. Nothing can equal the intensity of its attractions. It is one fifth of the atmosphere. It is three fourths of all animal bodies. It constitutes four fifths of every vegetable structure. Eight ninths of the weight of all the water is oxygen, and it is, so far as man has been able to determine, one half of the weight of the entire globe.

Now how is it that an element so *abundant* in the earth, and of such importance, is not found in the sun, if the sun is but the residual portion of that cosmical mass out of which the earth was taken? If one should say, because oxygen is a gas and being light, it was more easily cast off, we should reply, Why, then, do we still find a stratum of hydrogen of five to seven thousand miles in depth in the sun? Is not hydrogen lighter than oxygen?

But whatever may be the physical constitution of the sun, it is universally agreed that it is the chief source of light and heat, not only to the earth, but to all other planetary bodies. Moreover, it is agreed that but a small part of the light and heat radiated from the sun ever reaches the planets. Much the larger portion is dissipated in space.

Conceive of a spherical shell, one hundred and eighty-three millions of miles in diameter, with the sun at its center. Now conceive of a circular spot on the surface of this shell, whose area is equal to that of a great circle of the earth. What is the ratio of the area of this *spot* to that of the sphere itself? Such will be the ratio of the light and heat received from the sun by the earth, to the total radiation from the sun. From this it will be seen that the total radiation is more than two billion times as much as is received by the earth. It becomes, therefore, a question of universal interest, What is the *temperature* of the sun? If astronomers and physicists have been unable to agree as to the physical constitution of the sun, no more are they agreed as to its temperature.

There has been no lack of experiments on the sun's heat. Instruments and methods of measurement of the most diverse character have been employed. Estimates have been based on these experiments, and the result is, the estimates are irreconcilably discordant.

Sir John Herschell estimated that a solid shaft of ice, forty-five miles in diameter, plunged endwise into the sun at the rate of one hundred and ninety thousand miles per second, would be melted as fast as it entered. Sechi estimates the sun's temperature at two million degrees centigrade. Ericsson places it at six million to seven million degrees. But distinguished French physicists of the present day contend that it cannot exceed ten thousand degrees, and think it more likely that it does not exceed three thousand degrees.

Here is a wide range of opinions touching the temperature of the sun — from three thousand degrees to ten million degrees. The utmost that is *known* of this matter is that the sun is the source of heat as well as of light, and that the heat is immeasurable.

There is one other solar problem, and in some respects it is the most important of all. We know that the sun has furnished a sufficient supply of heat for long periods in the past, and that it furnishes a sufficient supply at present; but the question of *future* supply is one of so much interest that eminent physicists have devoted considerable labor to the settlement of it. But in its settlement they have proceeded from different premises. The first question which arises is, *What keeps up the solar temperature itself?*

Helmholtz assumes that the whole of the heat of the sun arises from the condensation of its mass. He says: " It may be calculated that if the diameter of the sun were diminished only the ten thousandth part of its present length, by this act a sufficient quantity of heat would be generated to cover the total omission for two thousand one hundred years." Dr. Sterry Hunt embraces substantially the same views. He says: " The sun, then, is to be conceived of as an immense mass of intensely heated gaseous and dissociated matter, so condensed, however, that, notwithstanding its excessive temperature, it has a specific gravity not much below that of water, [but the density of the sun is one and a half that of water,] probably offering a condition analogous to that which Cagniard De La Tour observed for volatile bodies when submitted to great pressure at temperatures much above their boiling point. The radiation of heat going on from the surface of such an intensely heated mass of uncombined gases will produce a superficial cooling, which will permit the combination of certain elements and the production of solid or liquid particles; these, suspended in the still dissociated vapors, become intensely luminous, and form the solar photosphere. The condensed particles carried down into the intensely heated mass, again meet with a heat of dissociation, so that the process of combination at the surface is incessantly renewed, *while the heat of the sun may be supposed to be maintained by the slow condensation of its mass.*"

But Professor Winchell distinctly repudiates the condensation theory, as follows: "*Conden-*

sation through loss of heat would create no tendency to increase the temperature, but condensation through the action of gravity would. The latter cause of condensation could only exist in a mass of matter temporarily out of the condition of molecular equilibrium, and could continue only while it is in the act of adapting its molecular state to the mechanical forces acting upon it.

"We are unable to state whether these forces vary in different regions and periods, and hence cannot safely assert that every, or any, nebulous body increases in temperature during any period of its history. *It seems more probable that a continuous reduction of temperature is experienced, and that the temperature inherent in the* sun at the present time is rather the residuum of the primordial heat than the effect of the condensation of his mass."

Professors Young, Tyndall, and others, advocate the meteoric theory of Mayer, and also the condensation theory of Helmholtz. Professor Young says: "The proper view is that the heat is maintained by the influx of matter. As meteors fall upon the earth, several millions in a day, so they fall into the sun, millions of millions per day, and contribute to the solar heat. But that does not account for it all. Another cause, I doubt not, is the contraction of its volume. If the sun were to contract one hundred and twenty feet in radius, or two hundred and forty feet in diameter, in a year, that would account for all the heat it gives off."

The meteoric theory of Mayer deserves a fuller exhibit. Perhaps no clearer statement of it has been made than that by Professor Thompson, who says: "In conclusion, then, the source of energy from which solar heat is derived is undoubtedly meteoric. The principal source, perhaps the sole appreciable efficient source, is in bodies circulating round the sun, at present inside the earth's orbit, in the sunlight by us called the zodiacal light. The store of energy for future sunlight is at present partly dynamical—that of the motions of these bodies round the sun—and partly potential—that of gravity toward the sun. This latter is being gradually spent, half against the resisting medium, and half in causing a continual increase of the former. Each meteor thus goes on moving faster and faster, and getting nearer and nearer the center, until some time, very suddenly, it gets so much entangled in the solar atmosphere as to begin to lose velocity. In a few seconds more it is at rest on the sun's surface, and the energy given up is vibrated across the district where it was gathered during so many ages, ultimately to penetrate as light the remotest regions of space.

Professor Tyndall, whether indorsing this meteoric theory directly or not, seems to give it countenance, and, following Helmholtz, generalizes in a most fascinating manner the history of the winding up of planetary affairs, as follows:—

"Solar light and heat lie latent in the force which pulls an apple to the ground. *The potential energy of gravitation was the original form of all the energy in the universe.* As surely as the weights of a clock run down to their lowest position, from which they can never rise again unless fresh energy is communicated to them from some source not yet exhausted, so surely must planet after planet creep in, age by age, toward the sun. When each comes within a few hundred thousand miles of his surface, if he is still incandescent, it will be melted and driven into vapor by radiant heat.* Nor if he be crusted over and become dark and cool externally, can the doomed planet escape its fiery end. If it does not become incandescent like a shooting star, by friction in its passage through his atmosphere, its first graze on his surface must produce a stupendous flash of light and heat. It may be at once, or it may be after two or three bounds, like a cannon shot ricochetting on a surface of earth or water, the whole mass must be crushed, melted, and evaporated by a crash, generating in a moment some thousand times as much heat as a coal of the same size would produce by burning."

Here is utterance sufficiently positive. If Tyndall were not a scientist, one might mistake him for a theologian of the old dogmatic type. One can scarcely resist the impression

---

* Prof. Tyndall ought to explain how the sun, which is not hot enough to be converted into vapor *itself*, can possibly convert a *planet* into vapor, while the said planet is yet " A few hundred thousand miles" away from "his surface." Is the *radiant* heat of the sun greater than the *resident* heat of the same body?

that the school of popular scientists are in danger of becoming dogmatical, especially on those questions that transcend their analysis.

It must be evident that the source of the sun's heat remains as uncertain as ever. Even the spectroscope, from which more has been expected than from all other instruments, gives us some equivocal answers, so that at one time we find that the sun has a solid or liquid nucleus, and at other times we are assured that it is gaseous. But neither spectroscope, telescope, or any other device, is able to inform us how the solar energy is maintained. Helmholtz, in the elation of an original thought, leaped to the conclusion that the condensation of the solar mass must maintain its temperature. Tyndall, with equal enthusiasm, follows. Both see the planetary mechanism running down. But Helmholtz is far less assured and dogmatic than his followers.

Thompson pronounces dogmatically on the zodiacal light, as if he knew what the zodiacal light is. It consists of meteors, he assumes, yet no astronomer has ever yet seen one of these meteors. No perturbations of Venus or Mercury or our moon has ever informed us of the existence of such a belt of meteors as is assumed. No one has ever seen any meteoric body, great or small, fall to the sun; and there are not wanting scientists of sufficient hardihood to explain the zodiacal light on principles which locate it in the earth's atmosphere, just as the rainbow is located on the cloud, both being effects of the reflection and refraction of the sunlight.

But what if the zodiacal light *be* the reflection of the sun's light from a nebulous ring, as Laplace supposed, does it follow that the sun is constantly devouring that ring, and thus maintaining its own heat? To us these speculations seem idle. Whence such a ring? Does the cosmical parent turn around and begin to devour his offspring as soon as it is born?

But let us return. It is strange that the advocates of the nebular hypothesis, who are so busy seeking out some way of accounting for the continued heat of the sun, do not see that the *original temperature* of the elements must have been the *highest* temperature to which they have ever been raised if the theory be allowed.

How do we know that? We answer: We know it, because the theory supposes all the matter of the solar system to have been in a state of gas—gas so attenuated that three cubic miles of it would have weighed only a single grain. Now what force can vaporize the elements but heat? And what heat is that which can convert them *all* into vapor? Now such a heat as would not only *vaporize* all the metals and metallic earths, but also attenuate their vapors to such an extent, is truly inconceivable. No such temperature exists in the solar system, or anywhere else, so far as we know, at the present time. Certainly no such heat exists in the sun, for the density of that body is 1.5. How many degrees of heat are necessary to convert the mass of this density into such a vapor as the original cosmical mass is supposed to have been? No one can fail to see that *Winchell is the only consistent theorist* among all that we have collated.

A "primordial heat," adequate to the expansion of the matter of the solar system to the volume required by the Nebular Hypothesis, would never need to be increased. We come to the conclusion, then, that if the nebular theory be accepted, all these theories of heat generation, whereby the solar temperature may be maintained, must be laid aside as irreconcilable with that theory.

True, the theories themselves are undemonstrated and undemonstrable. The only certain thing about them, when examined independently, is their uncertainty. But when examined upon the previously accepted Nebular Hypothesis, they cease to possess the least credibility. Let us, therefore, dismiss them, and consider the sun as cooling off. If the sun is cooling off and condensing, it must be obedient to the same law, in this respect, as any other of the bodies which were once a portion of its mass.

Let us, then, compare the sun with the earth, and see if we find them obedient to the same law, or if they now compare in the matter of density as they must compare if the theory be true.

At the time that the earth-mass is supposed by the theory to have been detached, the cosmical mass was a body having a diameter of one hundred and eighty-three millions of miles. Now, after detaching the earth, Venus, and

Mercury, it has shrunken to the diameter of eight hundred and fifty thousand miles. During that period its density must have become —making no allowance for the abstraction of Venus and Mercury—almost ten million times as great as it was at its beginning, because its volume *then* was about ten million times as great as its volume *now* is. But the earth has condensed three hundred and fifteen thousand times as fast as the sun, because the mass of the sun is three hundred and fifteen thousand times as great as that of the earth. The earth, then, must *now* be many thousand times as dense as the sun. But it is not. It is only about *four* times as dense as the sun.

It cannot be said that this is because the lighter matter was thrown off in the earth-mass, for we know that some of the heavier elements which are present in the earth are not detected in the sun, and that the lightest of all substances, hydrogen, is abundant in the sun. The relative densities of the sun and the earth are irreconcilable—so it seems to us—with the nebular theory.

It is conceded that there is an outer atmosphere of pure hydrogen enveloping the sun.

It is also universally agreed that there is a violent agitation of the chromosphere. Vast tongues of flame, many thousand miles high, have been observed. How is it possible, on the principle of the nebular theory, that such vast quantities (the hydrogen is five thousand to seven thousand miles in depth) have been retained in the sun, while many very heavy substances, such as platinum, silver, mercury, lead, tin, etc., were thrown off in the terrestrial mass? Tried by one postulate of the nebular theory, the sun is too light; tried by another postulate of the same theory, the sun is too heavy. Will the apostles of the theory come to the rescue of the sun?

CHAPTER XIII.

TEMPERATURE OF THE PLANETS.

IT must be borne in mind that the nebular theory is set forth as a history of planetary existence. It not only undertakes to account for the *origin* of the planetary masses, but it undertakes to explain the successive *stages* of planetary being. Leaving the original cosmical mass as a peripheral ring, each planetary mass is supposed to have cooled, contracted, granulated, and united in one body, which, assuming the spherical form, not only revolved around its original in an orbit, but also revolved on its own axis. And as, in the original mass, contraction by cooling produced an acceleration of the axial rotation, so in the planetary mass contraction, by cooling, produced an acceleration of the axial rotation until the planetary mass was enabled to detach peripheral rings, which became moons, and that all these bodies have gone on cooling and shrinking until now. Now it becomes, at least, a curious question, What is the present temperature of any one of these planets?

But in its relation to the credibility of the nebular theory this question becomes one of very grave importance, for, according to that theory, *five of these bodies are examples of successive stages of planetary history*, and give names to those stages. If, then, it shall appear that the temperature of each of these bodies is what the theory assumes it to be, it furnishes very strong confirmation of the theory as a whole. But, on the other hand, if it shall appear that these bodies do *not* exhibit the traces of such temperatures as are assigned to them respectively by the theory, then they give *no* testimony in favor of the theory.

Let the reader keep in mind the order of the history. The Saturnian stage is exemplified by the ring condition of Saturn; the Jovian stage, by the belted Jupiter; the terrestrial stage, by the habitable earth; the Martial stage, by the post-habitable Mars; and the lunar stage, by the frozen, shriveled, airless, and waterless moon. Such as these latter planets are supposed to be, such shall all other planets become, and such shall even the sun himself become at last.

This is history. Moreover, it is the custom of a *class* of scientists to speak of these things as among the *established truths* of modern science. Saturn, Jupiter, Mars, and the moon are represented as possessing certain physical peculiarities; these peculiarities are interpreted as the evidences of different temperatures, and the different temperatures mark the different stages of world history. If any one shall discredit this theory; if he shall question these assumed facts; if he shall speak of the possibility of different temperatures in different planets without the supposition of different successive stages of planetary history; if he shall set aside the hypothesis of original high heat and gaseous condition of all matter, he must expect to be denied the honor of scientific recognition himself.

According to the theory, the older the planet the cooler, provided that volume be equal to volume at the time of the formation of each. If at the time of detachment the planetary masses be of unequal volume, then the larger planet will continue at a high temperature longer than the smaller. There is another factor to be considered. Different substances conduct heat away, or, in other words, *cool off*, with different degrees of rapidity. The conducting power of silver is one hundred, while that of iron is but twelve.

Dry air is one of the poorest conductors. But we know that the effect of heat on air or gas is such as to throw it into violent agitation. The heated portions are sent to the surface, where its expanded substance is brought into contact with the intense cold, and thus the feeble conduction is compensated by the process of convection. Therefore we should conclude that a spherical mass of gaseous or aeriform matter, if it were launched into space at a high temperature, would very rapidly cool off by the process of convection. And if the elements composing the aeriform body were such as by condensation become solid, we should expect the period of solidity to approach rapidly. If this class of elements were present in small proportion, then we should find a small nucleus and an extended aeriform envelope, which would be permanent.

It is evident, then, that a planet might be of

very low specific gravity—that, for instance, of water—and yet not be very warm. Moreover, it is conceivable that a planetary nucleus may be *large* and *solid*, and yet be of low specific gravity.

The nebular theory assumes that the planetary masses commenced their independent career in the gaseous state, and it would require a great diminution of the temperature to bring the elements within the reach of the chemical forces. That a heat of dissociation exists in any of the planets is not claimed. But several of the metals do not need to be raised beyond liquefaction to dissociate them and regenerate each by itself pure. We may, therefore, conclude, that whatever elements are in the mass of any one of the planets, all the metals have now reached the stage of liquefaction or solidity, and whatever there remains of aeriform matter must be of the nature of an atmosphere surrounding this denser nucleus. But if the constitution of the more distant planets be similar to that of the earth, then can we account for their lightness without supposing them to be very hot?

We answer, first, that *we cannot account for*

their lightness by supposing them to be very hot. A heat sufficient to give such matter as constitutes the earth the specific gravity of Saturn, supposing that matter to be elementally distributed as it is in the earth, would make that matter incandescent. If, then, Saturn contain all the elements that are in the earth, and in the same proportions, the lightness of Saturn is inexplicable. Supposing it to be very hot would not explain it, unless we suppose it hot enough to render its nucleus incandescent. But that would be to render it a sun. It is a familiar fact that iron can be liquefied, and yet its specific gravity will be scarcely sensibly changed. When run into molds and cooled it does not shrink away from them so as to injure the cast which is formed. The same thing is observable of several other metals. It is also true of the metallic earths, that they may be raised to white heat, and yet their specific gravity is not greatly affected. If they shrank much in cooling the fabrication of symmetrical stone ware and porcelain would be impossible. How great must be that heat which, to any considerable degree, could lower the specific gravity of a planet! We repeat, it would be such that the planet would be a sun, shining with its own light.

We answer, secondly, We can account for the lightness of Saturn by supposing Saturn to be composed of light matter. As the elements are found unequally distributed on the earth, so it is not irrational to suppose that they may be unequally distributed among the planets. Winchell supposes it to be inevitable that in the formation of the planets by the process of detaching peripheral rings, the lighter matter would be in the outer planets. We confess to a degree of surprise when we find *him* explaining the lightness of Saturn on the supposition that it is very hot. Is it not better, even on the basis of the nebular theory, to suppose Saturn to be composed of very light matter?

There are not wanting, even in the earth, materials of sufficient lightness to build a comparatively light globe out of, if the architect choose to build it out of such material. Calcium is a light metal; so is aluminum. These two metals are the bases of most extensive formations on the earth. Magnesium, lithium, sodium, potassium, chlorine, are all light substances. Carbon, in its most dense form known to us, the diamond, is only three and a half times as heavy as water, and in other forms it is much lighter. Of the heavier metals, a less proportion may be supposed to be present, without in any way diminishing the stability of the structure. A solid globe, composed of light matter, may be surrounded with an atmosphere of much greater depth than one of the same magnitude composed of denser elements, yet the *density* of the atmosphere would not be excessive in its lower strata, because the density of the lower air is determined by the weight of the column, and the weight of the column is simply the measure of the total attraction of the mass upon it. If, then, the mass be specifically light, the attraction of a given volume will be proportionately light, and we may suppose that Saturn has a very deep atmosphere, and yet the supposition would not be incompatible with the supposition that Saturn is a habitable world. So much as to the possibilities in this case, without reference to the nebular theory.

Now let us look again at Saturn in the light of that theory. Saturn is quoted—so also is Jupiter—to show that the larger bodies cool off more slowly than the smaller bodies, and thus they exemplify different stages of history. Neptune is a large body, and, though it has been millions of ages cooling and condensing, it has only reached a point where its specific gravity is nine tenths. And Uranus is a large body, though not quite as large as Neptune, nor is it as old. It has not been so long cooling off. Yet its specific gravity is one. So much younger, and yet heavier! How is this? Why, don't you see? There are two reasons. First, the first planet was *composed of the lightest matter;* and, secondly, the first planet was the larger planet. Being the lighter matter, it never can become as heavy as the second will become; and, being the larger body, it cannot cool off so fast, and therefore the second body will condense the more rapidly. The fact is in exact accordance with the theory.

But what shall we say about Saturn? Its original density must have been much greater than that of Neptune, because the volume of the cosmical mass which threw off Neptune was thirty-eight and a half times as great as the volume of the same cosmical mass when it threw off the Saturnian mass. And yet Saturn is very light. Its specific gravity is only three fourths. But, it may be answered, Saturn is a very large body, and must cool off and condense more slowly on that account; and, besides that, Saturn is a much younger body than Uranus, and therefore has not had time to cool off so much, even if it were no larger. Very well, what kind of a body do you really think that Saturn is? An aeriform body? How? By the force of heat? Shall we allow that there are substances in Saturn which can become solid? Then they *are* solid now, or they are not. If they are solid, then they are in a condition in which the slowness of the process of cooling does not explain the lightness of Saturn, for we have shown that heat does not so expand the solids as to diminish their specific gravity to any considerable extent. But if they are aeriform by the action of heat, they are also incandescent. But Saturn is not an incandescent body. Saturn sheds from her broad disk a very mild reflected light. And there are indications of a dense atmosphere; and at the Saturnian poles are indications of snow and ice, which, in turn, indicate a solid globe and aqueous vapors in its atmosphere.

It would seem, then, that the temperature of Saturn cannot differ greatly from that of the earth. Thus in our cosmical equation we have the Saturnian stage = the terrestrial stage. It would seem that Saturn is destined to spoil the nebular theory by his inconsistences. He first *demonstrates* its truth by displaying a series of concentric rings above his equator. Then it is discovered that his rings are an illusion, and the demonstration is worthless. But his friends subsequently discover that the rings are simply granulated, and they take heart from the discovery. But, anon, it is found that his *levity* is altogether inconsistent with his age. But this is accounted for by the supposition, that being so great a body, he has not had time to cool off sufficiently to bring his density to the degree demanded by his relative position; and, last of all, this supposition is spoiled by the fact that he has a dense atmosphere filled with aqueous vapors, and that his polar regions are icy cold. Moreover, we are thus assured, that remote as he is from the sun, *his temperature is dependent on the solar influence;* for if the condition of his atmosphere depended on internal heat, it would be as warm at the poles as at the equator.

We see an adjustment of the planet's axis to his orbit, so that a succession of seasons is the result; we see an axial rotation producing day and night; we perceive an atmospheric temperature adapted to the absorption of aqueous vapors, which the spectroscope assures us are present in it; we see the indications of atmospheric changes similar to those with which we are familiar in the earth; and we behold the polar regions apparently covered with perpetual snow. All these circumstances concur in authorizing the inference that the thermometrical condition of Saturn so nearly resembles that of the earth that it may be the theater of similar vegetable and animal life, and may also be inhabited by beings whose constitution is similar to that of man.

From this examination of the indications of the condition of Saturn, and the bearings of them on the credibility of the nebular theory, we pass on to a similar consideration of the condition of Jupiter. "*The Jovian Stage*" of cosmical history is said to be exemplified by Jupiter. After describing, according to his conception of it, the condition of Mars, *Winchell* says: "When we lift our eyes to Jupiter, lying beyond the populous zone of asteroids, a strongly contrasted scene presents itself. Here are no outlines of continents and oceans, but only a series of changing belts, which are clearly phenomena of a medium of great mobility.

"It seems to be the general opinion that all we see of Jupiter is a perpetual envelope of clouds. These must float in an atmosphere at a very considerable elevation above the body of the planet, and thus occasion an exaggerated judgment of its bulk, and a diminished estimate of its density.

"How shall we explain this permanent envelope of watery vapor? The explanation is easy, for this is one of the phases which every planet must present in the progress of its cooling. A time arrives when the upper regions of the atmosphere first attain the temperature which condenses the vapor of water. During a cosmic period the clouds accumulate, slowly shutting out the light of the sun, and copiously discharging their rains toward the planet. The rains, penetrating the lower strata of the atmosphere, are converted to vapor, and returned to the clouds to be again condensed and precipitated. Every ascending particle of vapor carries off a portion of heat from the atmosphere, and promotes the cooling of the planet. But cosmic changes are slow, and ages must elapse while a tempest rages in mid air, which is quite unfelt upon the surface of the planet, save as the vivid lightnings shed a violet gleam over the arid surface, or the rolling thunders mark the time of the tempest's march. Gradually the line of conflict settles toward the heated crust. At length the rains strike the crust. Then, after a period of increased excitement in the elements, a universal ocean begins to accumulate—a boiling, steaming, turbid ocean. After a further lapse of ages the cooling and accumulating waters lead to signs of exhaustion in the clouds. Light filters feebly through, and the lowest organisms appear in the sea. Then the clouds break, and full sunlight and peaceful elements are the signal for advancing grades of organization.

"Such a scene has been witnessed in our own planet; such a storm seems to be raging to-day in the heavens of Jupiter. We gaze upon the shifting shadows of his long-drawn cloud belts; we imagine the tempest which is raging under their cover, and can almost fancy we see the cloudy mass lit up occasionally by an electric gleam.

"Here is a picture of an age long gone by in the history of the earth. Here is a stupendous object-lesson, which, like the curdled fire-mist which engirts the sun, demonstrates an ancient state of terrestrial things, to the knowledge of which men could not possibly attain either by history or tradition, or even the uncorroborated testimony of the rocks.

"Is it demanded how a planet so ancient as Jupiter can be in this condition, while Mars, earth, and Venus, so much younger, have long since passed their stormy epoch? We answer, the *mass* of Jupiter is so great that a larger period must be consumed in his refrigeration. The sun is older than the remotest planet, and has not yet attained even the stage of Jupiter. As Jupiter is a thousand times the volume of the earth, the sun is a thousand times the volume of Jupiter. The 'giant planet' seems hardly to have lost his inherent luminosity. He shines with a stronger light than could be expected, stronger than if his surface were covered with snow. He seems, indeed, to emit, as some think, even more light than he receives. Mars reflects but one fourth the light received from the sun, and the moon but one fifth. Even if, according to others, the light emitted by Jupiter is only three fifths as intense as total reflection of the solar light would render it, this, judging from the reflective capacity of Mars and the moon, implies that half his light is his own. Verily, the clouds must be in the earliest stage of condensation about this planet, or the lightnings are really producing such an illumination as in fancy we saw."—*Geology of the Stars.*

This is a vivid picture, sketched and colored by an artist of great ability and unbounded enthusiasm. And yet the picture is not entirely consistent, for certainly the existence of such an envelope of aqueous vapor as is capable of excluding the light of the sun, is inconsistent with a condition of luminosity in the planet itself. Clouds that can keep the light of the sun *out*, can quite as effectually keep the light of an incandescent planetary body *in*. We make no account of that lively fancy which invests the Jovian lightnings with the power to send their gleams to our earth. That evidently was an extravagant playfulness only. If, then, the planet Jupiter is really covered with dense aqueous vapors, it would seem to be conclusive that Jupiter is not sending to us any light that he does not reflect.

Now one of two things we will have to do: we shall have to spoil this "stupendous object-lesson" by dissipating these aqueous vapors, or we must extinguish a portion of that supposed excess of light which "implies that half his light is his own." Both suppositions cannot be accepted. Which shall be relinquished?

The true question, stripped of all irrelevant adorning, is simply this: Is Jupiter a self-luminous body, or is it not? Perhaps there is an overestimate of the *intensity* of the light of Jupiter.

Zolner, the distinguished Berlin astronomer and spectroscopist, has recently given much attention to celestial photometry. Employing a photometer of his own invention, by which he avails himself of the polarization of light, he is enabled to reach results of great definiteness and accuracy. He finds that the intensity of light reaching us from Jupiter is only $\frac{1}{3}$ as great as that of light reaching us from Venus, $\frac{7}{10}$ as great as that of light reaching us from Mars, and $\frac{1}{700}$ as great as that of the light of the moon. But Jupiter is about one thousand six hundred times farther off than the moon, and it would, therefore, require two million five hundred and sixty thousand moons to send us the amount of light from that distance that one moon sends from its present distance, were all shining with their own light.

But the disc of Jupiter has one thousand five hundred and forty-five times as much surface as the disc of the moon, and therefore Jupiter ought to give out one thousand five hundred and forty-five times as much light as the moon, and $1,545 \times 700 = 1,081,500$, the number of moons, at the distance of Jupiter, represented by the actual light of the moon. It will be seen, then, that the light which actually reaches us from Jupiter is such as to indicate an original intensity twice as great as that of the moon.

Does not this imply that half the light of Jupiter is his own? Not at all. When we estimate the amount of light that two convex mirrors will reflect to a given point there are three factors to be considered:—

1. Their respective distances from that object.
2. Their respective reflective powers.
3. Their respective convexities.

It is evident that when the mirrors are at different distances the reflected rays, which are not parallel, will be scattered over different spaces, and hence, within *given* spaces, will have different degrees of intensity. It is also evident that if one mirror reflect most of the light that falls on it, and another mirror *absorb* much of the light that falls on it, the two mirrors will reflect very different degrees of light to the same point. And it must also be evident that if one mirror be *very convex*, it will scatter most of the light, while a mirror of slight convexity will scatter comparatively little.

Now apply these three factors to the case of Jupiter and the moon as reflectors of light. Of the first we have already taken account.

Let us look at the second. What kind of surface makes the best reflector? Certainly that which is susceptible of the finest polish. But let the matter be full of indentations and projections, let the surface be rough, is it a good reflector? But all observers of the moon concur in representing its hither hemisphere as indescribably rough. It certainly is not a reflector of very high quality. If, on the other hand, Jupiter be enveloped by an atmosphere filled with aqueous vapor, it possesses a good reflective surface. Any one who has ever stood on a mountain and looked down on a lake of fog and witnessed the shimmer of the light reflected therefrom will remember its startling brilliancy. And he who has not seen this, may remember the glow of the cloud in the east made gorgeous by the rays of the setting sun. And all have seen the silver edge which the reflected rays of the sun put on the blackest thunder cloud.

If the atmosphere of Jupiter is filled with aqueous vapor, we can readily conceive that it must reflect so large a portion of the sun's rays that it should be the most glorious orb visible in the heavens at night. It does not need that we invent for Jupiter any luminosity to account for all the light he sends to us. But in our comparison of the moon and Jupiter we must not overlook their respective magnitudes. The diameter of Jupiter is eighty-five thousand miles. That of the moon is a little more than two thousand miles. The diameters are to each other as forty-two to one. Now a sphere three and a half feet in diameter will fairly represent Jupiter, and a sphere *one inch* in diameter will represent the moon. One half of the larger of these spheres will represent the reflecting surface of Jupiter, and half of the smaller will represent the reflecting surface of the moon. Behold the different degrees of convexity! No one, we think, can fail to see that parallel rays of light falling over an area equal to a hemisphere of the moon, on both planets would be reflected very differently by them. The rays that fall on the slightly convex surface of Jupiter would be thrown back in slightly divergent directions. But the rays that fall on the exceedingly convex surface of the moon must be dispersed widely in space. In this item of convexity Jupiter has great advantage as a reflector of the sun's light over Venus, Mars, and the moon.

To what conclusion do these facts conduct us? Evidently to this: notwithstanding the great distance of Jupiter, his light is not such as implies any thing but reflection. It is of no greater intensity than we have a right to expect it to be, considering his one thousand five hundred and forty-five lunar magnitudes of disc, his slight convexity of reflecting surface, and the excellence of his quality as a reflector of light.

That Jupiter is wholly opaque is further shown by the transits of Jupiter's moons. We see them not as we see Venus, where she makes a transit across the sun as a dark spot moving across a luminous disc, but as bright bodies, like the planet, yet casting a shadow on its disc as they cross.

Moreover, when these same moons pass on the opposite side of Jupiter we sometimes see them eclipsed by the planet. They enter his shadow, and emerge out of his shadow. But while they remain in his shadow there is no sign that he is serving as a sun to them in the slightest degree.

The telescopic features of Jupiter may be briefly enumerated. In the first place it appears to be destitute of continents and seas. If it has any extended, lofty ranges of mountains, astronomers have failed to detect them. It appears to be belted with clouds which are arranged parallel with the equator. These belts are sometimes apparently stationary for months, and sometimes they seem to break up, and to spread out over the whole disc of the planet.

Astronomers are generally agreed that the belts of Jupiter are phenomena of its atmosphere. The most convenient hypothesis is that they are "long-drawn cloud-belts," and that Jupiter is enveloped with a very deep, dense, and humid atmosphere, and that its very abundant vapors are, by the diurnal rotation, drawn out into parallel belts.

It would seem to be but a short step to the conclusion that the body of Jupiter must be very hot; that, in fact, a "universal, boiling, steaming, turbid ocean" is constantly discharging its steam into the atmosphere, and that the Jovian stage of planetary history, which is there receiving its exemplification, is a stage in which there is no possible life. A modern utilitarian might be pardoned a regret that so much steam power should be wasted. We venture a single suggestion: Is it not possible that the "long-drawn cloud-belts" of Jupiter are an optical illusion? Take an ordinary twelve-inch globe, and let it be revolved while you examine it. How moderate a motion is sufficient to render the images thereon indistinct, even while you stand over it! But remove from it twenty or thirty feet, and let its velocity be increased. What do you see? Continents, islands, mountains, oceans, seas, etc., run together in undistinguishable confusion. Even if the mountains were laid on, and the oceans dug out, so that irregularities proportionate to those on our globe were created, still, as the little globe revolves, what do you see? Do you not see belts? Are they not long drawn? Are they not parallel to the equator? Even so. And now if you only could manage to get up a half inch of atmosphere on this artificial globe, and have here and there a half-inch area of vapor floating in it, your long-drawn belts would be cloud-belts, would they not?

Let it be remembered, then, that stupendous as is the volume of Jupiter, its rotation is accomplished in less than ten hours. Thus the surface of Jupiter's equatorial zone sweeps by the observer at the rate of twenty-eight thousand miles an hour. What chance does this rush of the landscape afford for examining its features? Any observation made without a telescope of high power would be futile, for at his great distance from us no details could be made out. But if we could examine it with a power that would bring it apparently as near us as the moon is, the case would be little better, for the rotation would become sensible. This hypothesis is supported by the fact that all the changes of the Jovian aspects consist in a widening and narrowing of the belts. In other words, the observed atmospheric movements are in the direction of the poles. Is it possible that the clouds do not change their places to the east and west? But if they do, it would not, perhaps, be possible to perceive it.

That the changing aspects of the belts indicate changes in the relative position of cloud-masses we think not unlikely. Nor would it require a great excess of vapors in the atmosphere of Jupiter to answer the demands of our hypothesis. There is probably no day in the year when an observer of the earth from Venus or Mars would not see extensive fields of clouds in the earth's atmosphere, and it would not be strange if, as the earth revolves on its axis these fields of cloud should seem to be arranged in belts when there are no belts at all, though they would be moving only at the rate of one thousand miles an hour. And yet there is no universal tempest in the earth. The cloud-belts are all the indication that such a tempest is now "raging in the heavens of Jupiter." For aught we know the temperature of Jupiter is no higher than that of the earth, and it is sheer assumption to declare that "such a scene has been witnessed on this planet; such a storm seems to be raging to-day in the heavens of Jupiter."

But in the treatment of Jupiter, Winchell institutes a comparison with the sun. He asks: "Is it demanded how a planet so ancient as Jupiter can be in this condition, while Mars, earth, and Venus, so much younger, have long since passed their stormy epoch? We answer: the mass of Jupiter is so great that a larger period must be consumed in his refrigeration. The sun is older than the remotest planet, and has not yet attained even the stage of Jupiter. As Jupiter is a thousand times the volume of the earth, the sun is a thousand times the volume of Jupiter." These remarks suggest to us certain questions similar to those we have already raised touching Saturn. It is generally conceded that the density of Jupiter is about one and three eighths, while the density of the sun is one and a half. The sun is the denser body. And yet, according to Winchell's own reasoning, the planet, being only one thousandth the magnitude of the sun, it ought to have run through its cosmic periods with a thousand times the rapidity of the sun.

Why is the earth solid and cold, while Jupiter is boiling and steaming, and only beginning to harden? Why, bless you, that is not a hard question at all! Jupiter is a very great planet, and the earth is a very little one, and so the "mass of Jupiter is so great that a large period must be consumed in his refrigeration."

Well, the sun is a great body, too. It is a thousand times as large as Jupiter, is it not? And since it let Jupiter go out for himself the sun has been cooling off, has he not? And condensing? He has shrunken away from a magnitude indicated by the *orbit* of Jupiter himself to the *little* magnitude of the sun, a body whose diameter is only eight hundred and fifty thousand miles, has he not? You admit this. Well, then, what has this Jupiter been doing all this time? Cooling off! Indeed. And shrinking! Condensing! Does not your calculus say that he *must* have proceeded in this work a thousand times as rapidly as the sun? Then how is it that in the matter of condensing he has not even kept pace with the sun?

If the reasoning of Winchell be valid reasoning on this subject, Jupiter ought now to be hundreds of times as dense as the sun, unless we suppose it to have reached a condition in which its density cannot be increased by its cooling off. In that event the *Jovian stage* of planetary history would be dismissed, and the occasion would cease on which it could be said: "Here is a picture of an age long gone. by in the history of the earth. Here is a stupendous object lesson, which, like the curdled fire-mist which engirts the sun, demonstrates an ancient state of terrestrial things," etc.

All this, in the presence of sober inquiry, seems idle. Worse than idle! It is little less than charlatan dogmatism introduced into the domain of science.

"Curdled fire-mist that engirts the sun!" Curdled nonsense. If any dependence is to be placed on the revelations of the spectroscope, the sun is engirt *with very rare hydrogen gas.*

CHAPTER XIV.

PHYSICAL CONDITION OF MARS.

Telescopic appearance—Red land—Green seas—Seasons—Atmosphere—Clouds—Average temperature—Densities—Facts against theories.

THE planet Mars revolves around the sun at a mean distance of 139.3 millions of miles. Its diameter is about four thousand three hundred miles, or about twice that of our moon. Its diurnal rotation is accomplished in twenty-four hours, thirty-seven minutes, and twenty-two seconds. Its equatorial velocity is, therefore, a little more than five hundred and thirty miles an hour, or about $\frac{1}{32}$ of the equatorial velocity of Jupiter.

In several respects Mars is favorably situated for telescopic examination. Both at its conjunction with the sun and at its opposition it turns its illuminated hemisphere toward the earth, and although it passes through some of the phases of the moon, it always shows at least half of its disc enlightened. It is nearest the earth at its opposition, and then, like the full moon, shows a full, round disc. Its apparent magnitude is about fifty times as great at apposition as at conjunction, which circumstance renders that the most favorable time to observe it. It is also then in the darkest part of the heavens, and this circumstance gives us the full benefit of the planet's reflection.

Unlike the moon, Mars turns all sides successively to the observer, yet with a motion so deliberate as not to embarrass observation. Mars, to the naked eye, appears the ruddiest of all the heavenly bodies. Under the telescope it appears to be variegated, the principal colors being red, green, and white. Astronomers are generally agreed that the red portions are land, the green portions water, and the white portions, which are chiefly in the polar regions, are snow and ice. The divisions of red and green appear to be constant, as to each other, and so the supposition that they are permanent divisions of land and water seem to be justified. Which are land and which are water have been, and still continue to be, questions on which men speculate. The land may be red or reddish, like the red sandstone, some of the clays, and much of the feldspar of the earth. Some have imagined the existence of a Martial vegetation, the principal color of which is red. That even this is possible is evident from the existence on the earth of some species of plants, the stems and leaves of which are red.

But, on the other hand, it has not escaped notice that terrestrial waters have been found reddened by infusoria, and it has been thought that the waters of Mars may be reddened in the same manner, and so the red portions of that planet may be water and the green portions land. Then we might conceive of the land of that little planet as clothed in a garment of evergreen vegetation.

We may never be able to settle these questions. We might conceive that the Author of all things takes such delight in diversifying his works that the phenomena of land and water, and of vegetable and animal life upon that planet, shall be in strong contrast with kindred phenomena on the earth. But this is mere speculation. Are there any facts touching the physical constitution of Mars, which have been so well established that they are not considered doubtful by the leading astronomers of our times? Yes. It is not questioned that Mars is constituted of matter existing in the three forms, solid, liquid, and aeriform. It is chiefly a solid body. But there are bodies of water upon it, and it is surrounded by an atmosphere in which aqueous vapors are known to exist.

Janssen, of Paris, was at great pains to ascertain the spectrum of light which had passed through aqueous vapor. Afterward he made the planets Mars and Saturn the subject of spectroscopic observation, with special reference to the existence of aqueous vapors in their atmospheres, and he concluded that he had the proof of their existence.

Huggins has made the atmosphere of Mars a particular study, and he has found that the vapor of water exists there—true vapor of water—the same thing chemically as water on the earth. It follows, from these observations, that the average temperature of Mars cannot differ materially from that of the earth. The mass of the seas is fluid water. The temperature of the seasons depends on the relations of the polar hemispheres to the sun, and on nothing else. The sun has power to unlock the fastnesses of the ice-bound zones; to convert the snows of winter into the rivulets and brooks and swollen streams of spring and summer; to lift the aqueous particles out of the liquid state in the seas, and send them, on the wings of the wind, over the continents, where they are permitted to fall in showers of refreshing. There, as here, the great motive power is the sunlight, and it is sufficient when Mars is at its aphelion, and it is not in excess when, at his perihelion, he is thirteen millions of miles nearer the sun.

While Mars is thus constituted of solid, liquid, and aeriform matter, his specific gravity is $\frac{27}{100}$ of that of the earth. (Some place the specific gravity at four, water being one.)

We have been thus particular to state known features of the physical condition of Mars, because Mars is also a representative planet in the nebular theory. It exemplifies "the Martial stage." The Martial stage is a little in advance of the "terrestrial stage." Life, if it has not all gone out, is not very far from its last gasp in Mars, and the inhabitants of the earth may be assured that when the interior fires give out, the earth, too, will enter the Martial stage, and the final winter will commence. It may be some relief to recall Tyndall's comforting prediction that the earth will, after freezing up, fall into the sun, when it will certainly be hot enough for awhile. Will the reader pardon this pleasantry? We will proceed to sober work. In the discussion of the nebular theory in connection with Mars, we again assume as true the pertinent particulars of that theory.

That the planetary and solar matter originally existed in a gaseous condition; that the lighter matter went off in the outer planets; that all the planets have been cooling off and becoming more dense; and that the present condition of a planet depends, first, on its original density; second, on its original volume; and, third, on its age. If the matter of a planet consist of *elements* of low specific gravity, then, no matter what its age may be, the planet will be light. If the planet consist of *all* the elements which, in a dissociated gaseous state, were intermixed so as to make a *homogeneous mass*, as Sterry Hunt maintains, then the cooling and condensing will be attended with a regular increase of the specific gravity of the planet until it reaches the state of liquidity or solidity. If, then, the volume of one planet contracts exactly in the ratio in which the volume of another planet contracts, the densities of the two bodies being equal, each to each at the beginning, they will remain equal each to each through all the periods of their existence.

But if the original volume of one planet be twice or any number of times as great as the original volume of another planet, then, their original density being the same, the smaller planet will cool off and condense twice, or such number of times, as fast as the larger planet will cool off and condense.

Having assumed these principles as correct, we now beg the reader to accompany us in a careful and sober examination of this question, *What ought to be the comparative or relative densities of the earth, the moon, and Mars?*

Let us first compare the earth and Mars. If, as maintained by Hunt, the gaseous matter must be homogeneous, then we have the same elements in these three bodies. Mars, however, was the first to take his position and depart on his separate career. And Mars took only about one twenty-six hundred thousandth part of the paternal estate when he left; that is, the cosmical mass which Mars left behind was twenty-six hundred thousand times as great as the mass of Mars itself. Our nebular mathematics conducts us to the conclusion that the condensation of the Martial mass went on from that time twenty-six hundred thousand times as fast as the condensation of the parent mass. But in time, we know not how long, the parent mass shrunk to a magnitude indicated by the earth's orbit, and, at this time, it was still a gaseous mass, but its density was almost two and a half times what it was at the birth of Mars. Then the earth was detached, with a density almost two and a half times as great as the original density of Mars. But Mars was now two million six hundred thousand times as dense as at first. Therefore, when the earth began its planetary career, the density of Mars was more than a million times as great as that of the earth-mass. Now can the earth *ever* overtake Mars? No, not only because of the start which Mars actually had, but also because of the greater fleetness of Mars in the race. Mars is only about one eighth of the mass of the earth, and as to *volume* at the beginning of this contemporaneous history, Mars was only the one two million six hundred thousandth of his former self, while the earth was more than a million times larger than he. But as Mars is now only one eighth of the mass of the earth, he will cool off and condense eight times as fast as the earth can, and, therefore, the earth never can overtake him. Never. Even when Mars shall have reached that stage of refrigeration in which the whole mass is solid, if there be any degree of condensation still possible, Mars will progress faster than the earth can. But Mars has not yet reached that stage, and yet the earth has overtaken Mars and passed him in the race. The density of the earth is even now greater than the density of Mars. Mars ought to be frozen up. His seas and oceans ought to be absorbed by the rocks.

The Martial stage, according to Winchell, is one a *little further* advanced than the terrestrial stage. But Mars ought not to be in the Martial stage now, but in the *lunar* stage, if the principles of the nebular theory are applicable to him. Mars is, according to the theory, millions of years older than the earth. The earth is other millions of years older than the moon, and yet the moon is, according to the same theory, "a fossil world, an ancient cinder, suspended in the heavens, once the seat of all the varied activities which now characterize the surface of our earth, but in the present period a realm of silence and stagnation. Sprung from the bosom of the earth, there was a time when its physical condition had not diverged from that of the earth, but swung by itself in the midst of frigid space, *and having but one forty-ninth the bulk of the earth for the conservation of its temperature, cooling proceeded forty-nine times as rapidly as that of the earth. Its geological periods were correspondingly shorter.*"—*Geology of the Stars.*

Now we beg the advocates of this theory to adhere to its postulates. Why is the moon now a frozen planet, while the earth, which is its parent, continues internally molten, and is adapted externally for so many forms of life? Why? The answer is simple. The moon *was so little.* It was only one forty-ninth as large as the earth, and so it cooled off forty-nine times faster than the earth cooled, and that made its *"geological periods"* (not simply its "cosmic periods," while it was yet a gaseous body, but its geological periods also, all of them) correspondingly shorter. The lunar geological periods were only one forty-ninth as long as the terrestrial geological periods.

Very well. Now will you be so good as to tell us why Mars, which has only about one eighth as much mass as the earth, which at one time was only $\frac{1}{1000000}$ as *large* as the earth, which also is millions of years *older* than the earth, and which is hung out millions of miles farther in frigid space than the earth, has not yet frozen up? Why can we detect no real difference between the *temperature* of Mars and the temperature of the earth? We know of but one reason, and that is, we have no *theory* to serve by perceiving a difference where there is none, and where there are no signs of any.

The *mass* and *volume* of Mars being *small*, and the *age* of Mars being great, it ought, on the principles of the nebular theory, to be in the condition of the moon, but it is not. It is plump and fair, having oceans, seas, and an atmosphere, and showing all the signs of a physical condition similar to that of the earth.

Unless both planets have reached the point where their density does not change, the density of Mars ought to be greater than that of the earth. Thus Mars, both in temperature and in density, is an irreconcilable contradiction of the nebular theory.

CHAPTER XV.

PLANETARY MASSES.

ASSUMING the truth of the nebular theory, what will follow touching the *relative masses* of the planetary bodies? Shall we find them graduated by any law? Will they be equal each to each? Will the one first detached be least, and will each successive one be greater? Or will the first be greatest, and will each succeeding one be less than its immediate predecessor?

As a philosophical question we will consider not the actual, but the inevitable structure of the planetary system upon the assumption of the postulates of the Nebular Hypothesis and the operation of known physical laws.

We must not lose sight of the fact that the theory represents all the cosmical matter at the time of detaching a planetary mass as aeriform, the planetary mass itself as aeriform, and the elements as dissociated and mixed intimately together. And while one class teach that the lighter elements were in the outer portions, another class teach that they were so intermixed that the mass was homogeneous. It must also be borne in mind, that according to the hypothesis, the planetary matter was detached as a peripheral ring, and afterward became a planet. The peripheral ring was detached by the centrifugal force, but how the ring was changed into a planetary mass the advocates of the theory do not try to show. Touching the centrifugal force, we know that it arises out of the rotary motion, and that it may be productive of great effects.

But we know also that whenever a body is moved a *certain amount* of force is exerted. So, also, whenever the direction of the motion of a body is changed a *certain amount* of force is exerted. We may never be able to determine *what amount* of force would be requisite to produce the first peripheral ring; but one thing we may confidently say, that if two bodies of the same size and density were revolving in space, then, whatever velocity of rotation in one of them would cause the detachment of a peripheral ring, exactly the same velocity in the other would also detach a peripheral ring. But that is to say that a fixed ratio must exist between the centrifugal force and the quantity of matter which it is able to detach under the same conditions.

Against the centrifugal force two other forces are acting. The force of cohesive attraction, though infinitely feeble, may be said to exist in the gaseous substance. The force of gravity on the peripheral portion of the mass can be estimated by assuming the distance which the periphery was from the center, and assuming the quantity of matter in the mass.

But it may also be estimated relatively for any two or more peripheral rings by simply assuming the distance. Let G be the force of gravity at the distance of Neptune. Then, as this force is inversely as the squares of the distances, it will be at the distance of Uranus, about 3 G; at the distance of Saturn, 11.5 G; at Jupiter, 36.9, etc. It will be seen, then, that the centrifugal force will have three times as much gravitative force to overcome at the distance of Uranus as at the distance of Neptune. At the distance of Saturn it will have eleven times as much, and at the distance of Jupiter thirty-six times as much. And this will go on so long as the cosmical mass continues to contract. In each case of ring detachment, so much matter as the ring contains will transfer its gravitative influence to the outer regions. If it continue a *ring*, its pull on the peripheral portion of the mass will be uniform on all sides, and will counteract an equal inward gravitation. But if it be assembled into a planetary mass its pull will be all in one direction, and we may conceive that it will assist in breaking up future rings. But the gravitative force which the mass of Neptune could exert when *near* the periphery can be only $\frac{1}{20,000}$ G, and it will constantly diminish as the mass contracts, so that at the time of the detachment of the Uranian mass it will not exceed $\frac{1}{1,000,000}$ G, an element of influence too minute to greatly affect the results, and we will, therefore, omit further reference to these separate counteracting attractions. We shall see that the centrifugal force, before it could detach matter from the periphery of the rotating sphere—assuming that it could detach at all—must, in each instance, as we proceed toward the center, overcome a gravitative force several times greater than it overcame in the next preceding instance. And the same thing must be true of density. If the density of the mass will have any modifying power, it will certainly be increased as the mass contracts and the density increases. We shall then conceive of the cosmical sphere as rotating with accelerated velocity, until it reaches the point at which the feeble coherency of the substance and the powerful attraction of the mass upon the protuberant equator are overcome by the centrifugal force, and this equatorial portion is lifted off as a ring. We now conceive of a gradual contraction of the mass, by which its density is made four and a half times as great as at first, and the central gravitation of the periphery is become three times as great as at first. In thus contracting, the rate of axial rotation has been increased from $\frac{25}{100,000}$ of a degree per hour to $\frac{49}{100,000}$ of a degree per hour, that is, the rate of axial rotation as nearly doubled.

At this point the Uranian planetary mass is detached, and again the parent mass contracts until its density becomes about thirty-eight times as great as at first, and the gravitative force holds the peripheral matter more than eleven times as strongly as it did at first, and at this time the axial rotation has increased to $\frac{1.4}{10,000}$ of a degree per hour, that is, it is 5.6 times as great as at first. And now the ~~Ura~~-nian mass is separated from the parent mass. Again, there is gradual contraction until the density is two hundred and forty times as great as at first, the central gravitative force is more than thirty-six times as great upon the peripheral matter as it was at first, and the axial rotation is $\frac{3.4}{10,000}$ of a degree per hour, or 3.6 times as great as it was at first, and then the Jovian mass is detached.

We need not extend this exhibit further. We now proceed, on the presumption that we know absolutely nothing about the actual masses of these several planets. We will reason from the known fact that a double force will be required to overcome double resistance. We know that the centrifugal force is quadrupled if we double the rate of rotation. We also know that the force of gravity is quadrupled if we diminish the distance to one half.

It may be assumed, then, that the increase of the velocity caused by contraction will be exactly offset by the increase of the gravitative force arising from the same cause, and we leave it out of our calculation. What, then, will happen? Will the second ring contain more matter than the first, or will it contain less, or will it be just the same?

There is one element to be considered as likely to modify the result. That element is density. We can hardly conceive that the change of density will not, in some way, affect the detaching efficiency of the centrifugal force. But so long as the changes of density are all in one direction, the effect of density on the detaching efficiency will be in one direction.

Let it be assumed that increase of density will hinder the detaching force, so that it cannot throw off so large a mass. Then the second planetary mass will be less than the first, the third less than the second, the fourth less than the third, and so on to the last. Then the outmost planet will be greatest, and the innermost one will be least. And *if there be any law governing the formation of these hypo-*

thetical rings, *then we shall find a regular gradation of planetary masses*, the planet of least mass being nearest the sun.

But, on the other hand, let it be assumed that the increase of density will so *increase* the efficiency of the centrifugal force that it will carry off a *larger* portion of the peripheral matter. The second planetary mass will be larger than the first, the third larger than the second, the fourth larger than the third, and so on, until the last will be found the largest of all. Here, again, will be a regular gradation; but the remotest planet will be least, and the "giant planet" will be found nearest the sun.

Is it too much to say that this regular gradation of the planetary masses is one of the "uniformities" which we are authorized by the fundamental postulates of the nebular theory to expect? No matter which way the gradation is, from greater to less or from less to greater, would it not seem to be a theoretical necessity?

We speak thus confidently, because it is well known that velocities and forces have mathematical relations. Problems of *force*, in which *matter* and *motion* are the factors, are of almost daily occurrence.

We are now prepared to make one more survey of the planetary system, and examine the actual relative masses of the planets. We take account not of volume, because that is supposed to be undergoing change. We take account of *masses*, because these are constant, and we will employ, as the unit of our scale, the mass of the earth. With the earth as one, we find Neptune sixteen and one half. It is a large planet. We conclude that the extreme tenuity of the cosmical stuff was favorable to the formation of large planets. We pass on to Uranus. It is found to be only about three fourths as large as Neptune. How shall we explain this falling off? It cannot be for the lack of velocity, because that has almost doubled. But the density has increased fourfold. It must be that. And as we know that the density will increase as the volume contracts, we conclude that the planetary masses will be found to be less and less as we proceed toward the sun.

Let us go forward and verify our generalization. We find the orbit of Saturn, and we

Planetary Masses. 285

know that in contracting to the limit marked by this orbit the density of the cosmical stuff is made eight times as great as it was when Uranus was detached, while the rate of the axial rotation is only two and eighty-five one hundredth times as great as it then was. So great an increase of density and so small an increase of velocity! Surely the new planetary mass must be very small! Amazing futility of deduction!

Look at the Saturnian mass. In our scale it stands at ninety earth-masses. It is seven times as great as the Uranian mass. Capricious Saturn! The gradation is reversed. We are on an ascending scale.

Let us examine Jupiter. The gradation is precipitous. Jupiter exhibits a mass equal to three hundred and one earths. It is more than three times as great as Saturn. And yet the density of the fire-mist, out of which the Jovian mass is supposed to have been taken, was six and a half times as great as that of the Saturnian mass, and *two hundred and forty-seven* times that of the original world-stuff.

Our comparison of the planetary masses does not give satisfactory results. At first it suggests that the increase of density in the revolving mass will so embarrass the efficiency of the centrifugal force that it will detach less and less matter from its periphery. But again and again it has seemed to show that it will cause it to detach *larger* masses successively. So now we must conclude, contrary to our first conclusion, that the planets will be found larger and larger as we proceed toward the sun. We still insist that if this be the mode in which the worlds have been formed, we must find some uniformity in the effects of the centrifugal force.

There *is* a mathematical ratio between motion and force, so that if a given amount of matter be moved with different velocities there will be an ascertainable amount of force which each respective velocity will generate. And there is a mathematical ratio between matter and force, so that with the same *motion* different quantities of matter will exert correspondingly different degrees of force. And if rings could be detached at all from the hypothetical cosmical sphere there must be a law governing the operation.

Just here we insist on finding one of the

"marvelous unformities," but thus far we have found marvelous diversities and discrepancies instead. Will they continue? We were following the gradation of planetary masses, and found ourselves on an ascending scale. We pass from Jupiter to Mars. What an abrupt reversal of the order! The *gradation* is utterly destroyed. Jupiter is equal to twenty-four hundred such bodies as Mars.

The density of the cosmical matter out of which Mars was separated was twenty-seven times as great as that out of which Jupiter came. But the rate of the axial rotation was six times as great. What, then, is the cause of this falling off in effects?

It seems inexplicable. There is now the highest rate of motion that there has even been, and yet here is the smallest product. It seems to say that there is no ratio existing between the alleged force and the alleged effect. In one case the increase of density and increase of velocity result in a diminished product. In the next case a further increase of density and a further acceleration of velocity result in a product several times greater. In the next case a further increase of density and a further acceleration of velocity result in a still greater product. But in the next case, with the increase of density and acceleration of velocity, there is the merest fraction of the last result.

We have passed over the asteroids. They would exhibit the same startling disparity between the force employed and the work accomplished. Coming on to the earth, we see another reversal of the order. The velocity is greater, the density is greater, and the result is greater. But again it is reversed at Venus. There, again, the velocity is greater and the density is greater, but the result is less. And thus we are compelled to pronounce again, "There appears to be no philosophy in this nebular theory."

That the peripheral portion of an aeriform body could be cast off at all by the centrifugal force has never been shown. But if there be a point in the acceleration of the velocity of a rotating aeriform body at which the centrifugal force is a detaching force, that point must be mathematically fixed, though we may not know where it is. But if it be fixed, the same force acting on the same matter under the same conditions will produce the same uniform effects. If the condition of the matter change, and the velocity of the motion remain unchanged, and all the other conditions remain unchanged, then if the result be changed we can only account for it by alleging the change in the condition of the matter. Such a change is the increase of density.

We know that the increase of velocity cannot diminish the centrifugal force, but must increase it. Increase of force must increase production, unless there be a corresponding increase of resistance. If the increase of density *be* such corresponding increase of resistance, we cannot account for the tremendous masses of Saturn and Jupiter. If the increase of density be *not* such corresponding increase of resistance, we cannot account for the *smallness* of the masses of Mars, Earth, Venus, and Mercury. In any event we cannot reconcile the inconstancy of results with the known facts of motion and density.

The actual masses of the planets are not what they must be if they were produced by the centrifugal force out of a revolving mass of aeriform matter. We were assured that marvelous uniformities existed, but we have found unaccountable diversities. The supposed uniformities were considered a powerful argument for the nebular theory. What *do* the unaccountable diversities show?

We are obliged to conclude that the nebular theory lacks all the elements of credibility. It is at variance with astronomical facts. It is destitute of philosophical consistency. It assumes every thing that ought to be demonstrated. It deals in "glittering generalities" where it ought to go into minute details. It ignores the mathematical relation of forces and effects. In fine, its data are intangible, incongruous, and impertinent to its conclusions. Never in the history of science was theory more pretentious. Never did theory less justify its pretension.

It has unquestionably the patronage of great names, so that it may seem to be unthinking temerity to challenge it. Nor have we done so hastily. A somewhat careful study of the subject for thirty years has only deepened our conviction of the worthlessness of the theory as a history of the origin of worlds.

We have read with candid interest the expositions of it given by its advocates. With them we have hailed with pleasure the new discoveries that were supposed to shed light on the subject. But we have been constantly amazed to see how much learned men will take for granted, and how little they will feel the force of great *facts* when they glance at them through the colored medium of a theory. We have the profoundest respect for men of scientific culture. They are the honored leaders of public thought. We would not pluck a single garland from the brow of one of these men. But we know of no infallibility. And that dogmatic dictum which imposes a religious faith and anathematizes all who dissent, is no more repulsive and monstrous than the equally dogmatic prescription of crude and extravagant fancies under the fascinating caption of Popular Science.

If assumptions were demonstrations, then would the nebular theory be demonstrated. If confident assertion were the test of credibility, then we must confess that the theory is credible. The one thing in which its advocates excel is florid rhetoric. Their writings glow with imagery of transcendent beauty, and it is not strange that in "Popular Science" it has the chief place assigned it. As a theory of development it may properly precede that of Darwin touching living forms. Unsupported itself, it can only leave that to be examined on its own independent merits.

Winchell says of the nebular theory: "This doctrine has earned unquestioning acceptance simply because it accords with all the phenomena."

We have shown that it accords with few, if any, of the phenomena.

Again, Winchell says: "Occasionally we hear a dissenting voice, but it proceeds, almost always, from persons who, whatever their eminence in theology or letters, have little authority in matters of scientific opinion."

We refer to this remark for one purpose only, and that is to say, we do not wish any man to rest in our opinions. We have undertaken to look at facts as they are in nature. We announce no opinions except as the facts seem to point. We invite a consideration of the arguments based on the facts, without regard to any theological or other than scientific results. Let us know the truth as nature herself teaches the truth. If any theology cannot abide the truth, let it suffer. We shall shed no tears for it. *We quote no book against the nebular theory but the open volume of nature. We urge against it no laws that we find not in nature's code.*

INDEX.

Arago, views respecting recent lunar eruption, 196.
Artesian wells, temperature of, at different depths, 168.
Asteroids, what ? 76.
    " great number of, 101.
    " Pallas, inclination of the orbital plane, 101.
    " masses of, 288.

Centrifugal force, defined, 63.
    "   " ratio of, to rate of motion, 63.
    "   " direction of, 92.
    "   " effect of, on a sphere, 65.
Comets, theoretical origin of, 101.
    " direction of the motion of, 102.
Cosmical History, tentative exhibits of, 31.

Density of the original nebulous sphere, 38.
    " of the planets, 117.
    " theoretical gradation of, 120.
    " original, relative, of the planets, 123.
    " of Neptune and Uranus compared, 126.
    " of Uranus and Saturn compared, 127.
    " of Saturn and Jupiter compared, 128.
    " of the sun and the earth compared, 232.
    " effect of, on ring formation, 282.

Earth, condition of its interior, 153.
    " views of Hunt, Hopkins, and Scrope, 184.
    " views of Lyell, 159.
    " views of Poisson, 161.

Gradation, theoretical, of densities, 120.
    "   theoretical, of planetary masses, 276.

Hopkins, on the thickness of the earth's crust, 170.
Herschell, Sir William, discovery of nebulæ, 18.
    "   "   respecting the sun, 213.
Herschell, Sir John, on the temperature of the sun, 222.
Helmholtz, on the maintenance of the sun's heat, 35.
    "   on the density of the original nebulous sphere, 38.
    "   on the original motion of rotation, 44.
    "   on the original store of force, 138.
Hunt, Sterry, on first chemical combinations, 145.
    "   "   on chemical relations of intensely heated matter, 42.

Kirchhoff, on the physical constitution of the sun, 215.

Lockyer, on the physical constitution of the sun, 218.

Moon, present condition of the, 197.
    "   motions of, 200.
    "   temperature of, 204.
    "   occultation of Jupiter by, 204.

Nebulæ, discoveries of, 17.
    "   classified by Herschell, 18.
    "   sun through Lord Ross's telescope, 19.
Nebular theory, statement of the, by Winchell, 22.
    "   "   statement of the, by Wells, 24.

Orbital periods of the planets, a clew to the original axial rotation, 78.
    "   "   constancy of, 79.

Planetary motions, rate of, 87.
    "   "   direction of, 88.

INDEX. 297

Planetary motions, irreconcilable with nebular theory, 109.
Plateau, interesting experiment of, 59.

Rings, theory of formation of, Winchell, 55.
" discussion of the theory, 57.
" of Saturn, an optical illusion, 59.
Rotary motion in the solar system, 36.
" " theory of the origin of, Winchell, 22.
" " theory of the origin of, Wells, 28.
" " theory of the origin of, Spencer, 52.
" " original must be assumed, 44.

Satellites of Uranus and Neptune, 103.
Schellen, elements present in the sun, 219.
Sechi, conjecture of, respecting aqueous vapor in the sun, 218.
Sun, situation of, as center of the planetary system, 100.
" volume and mass of the, 210.
" axial rotation of the, 97.
" proper motion of, in space, 76.
" physical constitution of the, 211.
" temperature of, how maintained, 223.
" elements present in the, 219.

Temperature, defined, 147.
" of original world stuff, Winchell, 22.
" of original world stuff, Helmholtz, 139.
" of the sun, how maintained, 223.
" increase of, in mines and wells, 165.
Tyndall, on the original energy, 44.
" on the destiny of planets, 227.

Velocities, actual, in the solar system, 75.
" table of, 80.

Wells, David A., statement of nebular theory, 24.
" " on the internal condition of the earth, 169.
Wells, artesian, temperature of, at different depths, 168.

Whirlpool, theory of the, 45.
Wilson, views of, respecting the sun, 213.
Winchell, statement of nebular theory, 22.
" tentative exhibit of cosmical history, 31.
" theory of ring formations, 55.
" theory of the sun, 225.

Young, views respecting a liquid solar crust, 219.

Zodiacal light, 230.

Publications of Nelson & Phillips,
805 Broadway, N. Y.

Butler's Analogy of Religion. With a Life of the Author. Edited by Rev. Joseph Cummings, D.D., LL.D., President of Wesleyan University. 12mo. Price, $1 75.

From Atheism to Christianity. By Rev. Geo. P. Porter. 16mo. Price, 60 cents.

The Great Conflict. Christ and Antichrist. The Church and the Apostasy. By Rev. H. Loomis. 12mo. Price, $1.

Philosophy of Herbert Spencer. Being an Examination of the First Principles of his System. By B. P. Bowne, A.B. 12mo. Price, $1 25.

Love Enthroned; or, Essays on Evangelical Perfection. By Daniel Steele, D.D. 12mo. Price, $1 50.

Methodism and its Methods. By Rev. J. T. Crane, D.D. 12mo. Price, $1 50.

Star of Our Lord; or, Christ Jesus King of all Worlds, both of Time or Space. With Thoughts on Inspiration, and the Astronomic Doubt as to Christianity. By Francis W. Upham. 12mo. Price, $1 75.

The Wise Men. Who they Were: and How they Came to Jerusalem. By Francis W. Upham, LL.D. 12mo. Price, $1 25.

Meditations on the Actual State of Christianity. By M. Guizot. 12mo. Price, $1 75.

Meditations on the Essence of Christianity. By M. Guizot. 12mo. Price, $1 75.

Misread Passages of Scripture. By J. Baldwin Brown. 12mo. Price, 75 cents. Second Series, price, $1.

Mission of the Spirit; or, The Office and Work of the Comforter in Human Redemption. By Rev. L. R. Dunn. 12mo. Price, $1 25.

Mystery of Suffering, and other Discourses. By E. De Pressensé, D.D. 12mo. Price, $1 25.

Principles of a System of Philosophy. An Essay toward Solving some of the More Difficult Questions in Metaphysics and Religion. By A. Bierbower, A.M. 12mo. Price, $1 25.

Publications of Nelson & Phillips,
805 Broadway, N. Y.

AYESHA. A Tale of the Times of Mohammed. By Emma Leslie. Illustrated 12mo. Price, $1 50.

FLAVIA; or, Loyal to the End. A Tale of the Church in the Second Century. By Emma Leslie. Illustrated 12mo. Price, $1 50.

GLAUCIA. A Story of Athens in the First Century. By Emma Leslie. Illustrated. 12mo. Price, $1 50.

LEOFWINE, THE SAXON. A Story of Hopes and Struggles. By Emma Leslie. Illustrated. 12mo. Price, $1 50.

ELFREDA. A Sequel to Leofwine. By Emma Leslie. Illustrated. 12mo. Price, $1 50.

QUADRATUS. A Tale of the World in the Church. By Emma Leslie. Illustrated. 12mo. Price, $1 50.

SUNSHINE OF BLACKPOOL. By Emma Leslie. Price, $1.

HOPE RAYMOND; or, What is Truth. By Mrs. E. J. Richmond. Illustrated. Large 16mo. Price, $1.

THE TWO PATHS. By Mrs. E. J. Richmond. Price, $1.

MEHETABEL. A Story of the Revolution. By Mrs. H. C. Gardner. Illustrated. Large 16mo. Price, $1 25.

MORAG; a Story of Highland Life. 12mo. Price, $1 25.

MOTHER, HOME, AND HEAVEN. A Collection of Poems. Edited by Mrs. J. P. Newman. Square 18mo. Gilt edge. Price, $1 50.

DEWDROPS AND SUNSHINE. A Collection of Poems about Little Children. Edited by Mrs J. P. Newman. Square 18mo. Gilt edge. Price, $1 50.

JACQUELINE. A Story of the Reformation in Holland. By Mrs. Hardy. Four Illustrations. 16mo. Price, 80 cents.

LUCIEN GUGLIERI. By Mary B. Lee. 16mo. Price, 60 cents.

LILIAN. A Story of the Days of Martyrdom in England Three Hundred Years ago. 16mo. Price, 90 cents.

Publications of Nelson & Phillips,
805 Broadway, N. Y.

ARCTIC HEROES. Facts and Incidents of Arctic Explorations. From the Earliest Voyages to the Discoveries of Sir John Franklin, embracing Sketches of Commercial and Religious Results. By Rev. Z. A. Mudge. Illustrated. 12mo. Price, $1 25.

NORTH-POLE VOYAGES. Embracing Sketches of the Important Facts and Incidents in the latest American Efforts to reach the North Pole, from the Second Grinnell Expedition to the Polaris. By Rev. Z. A. Mudge. 16mo. Price, $.

THE SQUIRE OF WALTON HALL; or, Sketches and Incidents from the Life of Charles Waterton, Esq., the Adventurous Traveler and Daring Naturalist. By Daniel Wise, D.D. Six Illustrations. Price, $1 25.

JOHN WINTHROP AND THE GREAT COLONY; or, Sketches of the Settlement of Boston and of the more Prominent Persons connected with the Massachusetts Colony. By Charles K. True, D.D. Price, $1.

SUMMER DAYS ON THE HUDSON. The Story of a Pleasure Tour from Sandy Hook to the Saranac Lakes, including Incidents of Travel, Legends, Historical Anecdotes, Sketches of Scenery, etc. By Daniel Wise, D.D. Illustrated by 109 Engravings. Price, $2.

GEMS OF INDIA; or, Sketches of Distinguished Hindoo and Mahomedan Women. By Mrs. E. J. Humphrey. Illustrated. 12mo. Price, $1 25.

SIGHTS AND INSIGHTS; or, Knowledge by Travel. By Rev. Henry W. Warren. Illustrated. 12mo. Price, $1 25.

GLIMPSES OF OUR LAKE REGION IN 1863, and other Papers. By Mrs. H. C. Gardner. 12mo. Price, $1 50.

SIX YEARS IN INDIA; or, Sketches of India and its People, as seen by a Lady Missionary, given in a Series of Letters to her Mother. By Mrs. E. J. Humphrey. Eight Illustrations. 12mo. Price, $1 25.

LIVINGSTONE IN AFRICA. By Rev. S. A. W. Jewett. 12mo. Price, $1 50.

Publications of Nelson & Phillips,
805 Broadway, N. Y.

Discontent, and other Stories. By Mrs. H. C. Gardner. 12mo. Price, $1 25.

Little Foxes. By the Author of "How Marjorie Watched." Illustrated. Large 16mo. Price, 90 cents.

Helena's Cloud with the Silver Lining. By the Author of "How Marjorie Watched," etc. Price, 90 cents.

Little Princess, and other Stories, Chiefly about Christmas. By "Aunt Hattie." 18mo. Price, 65 cents.

Peter the Apprentice. An Historical Tale of the Reformation in England. 16mo. Price, 90 cents.

Romance Without Fiction ; or, Sketches from the Portfolio of an Old Missionary. By Rev. Henry Bleby. 12mo. Price, $1 75.

Dora Hamilton ; or, Sunshine and Shadow. 16mo. Price, 90 cents.

Dying Saviour and the Gipsy Girl. 18mo. Price, 50 cts.

Bessie and Her Spanish Friends. By the Author of "Faithful, but not Famous," etc. 16mo. Price, 90 cents.

Ben and Bentie Series. School Life of Ben and Bentie. Price, 90 cents. Camp Tabor. Price, 90 cents.

True Stories of the American Fathers. For the Girls and Boys all over the Land. By Miss Rebecca M'Conkey. Illustrated. 12mo. Price, $1 50.

Martyrs of the Catacombs. 16mo. Price, 90 cents.

Anna Lavater. A Picture of Swiss Pastoral Life in the Last Century. By Rev. W. Ziethe. 12mo. Price, $1.

A Visit to Aunt Agnes. Illustrated. Tinted. Square 12mo. Price, $1.

Suzanna De L'Orme. A Story of Huguenot Times. 12mo. Price, $1 25.

Talks with Girls. By Augusta Larned. 12mo. Price, $1 50.

Story of a Pocket Bible. Illustrated. 12mo. Price, $1 25.

True Stories of Real Pets ; or, Friends in Furs and Feathers. Illustrated. Square 16mo. Price, $1 25.

Rosedale. A Story of Self-Denial. By Mrs. H. C. Gardner. 12mo. Price, $1 75

Publications of Nelson & Phillips,
805 Broadway, N. Y.

Renata of Este. From the German of Rev. Carl Strack. By Catherine E. Hurst. 12mo. Price, $1 25.

The Little Trowel. By Edith Waddy. Illustrated. Large 16mo. Price, 90 cents.

Story of a Pocket Bible. Illustrated. 12mo. Price, $1 25.

Half Hours with Old Humphrey. By George Mogridge. 12mo. Price, $1.

John Richmand; or, a Sister's Love. By T. Taylor. Illustrated. 12mo. Price, $1.

Fraulein Mina; or, Life in an American German Family. By Miss Mary H. Norris. 12mo. Price, $1 25.

Round the Grange Farm; or, Good Old Times. Stories of Scottish Life. By Jean L. Watson. Six Illustrations. 12mo. Price, $1 25.

Shepherd-King. By A. L. O. E. Illustrated. 12mo. Price, $1 25.

My Sister Margaret. By Mrs. C. M. Edwards. Illustrated. 12mo. Price, $1 25.

Stony Road. A Scottish Story from Real Life. 12mo. Price, 85 cents.

Sunday Afternoons. A Book for Little People. By E. F. Burr, D.D. 16mo. Price, 75 cents.

Temptation and Triumph. By Virginia F. Townsend. Revised. 12mo. Price, $1 25.

My Uncle Toby. His Table Talks and Reflections. By an Attorney-at-Law. Large 16mo. Price, $1 25.

Victoria, with other Poems. By S. I. Henry. 12mo. Price, $1.

Village Blacksmith. 18mo. Price, 75 cents.

Winter at Woodlawn; or, the Armor of Light. Illustrated. Square 16mo. Price, 90 cents.

Royal Road to Fortune. By Emily H. Miller. Illustrated. 12mo. Price, $1 50.

Simple Stories with Odd Pictures; or, Evening Amusements for the Little Ones. With Twenty Illustrations. By Paul Konewka. 16mo. Price, 75 cents.

Through the Dark to the Day. A Story. By Mrs. Jennie F. Willing. 12mo. Price, $1 50.

www.ingramcontent.com/pod-product-compliance
Lightning Source LLC
Chambersburg PA
CBHW031249250426
43672CB00029BA/1418